The Writing Workshop

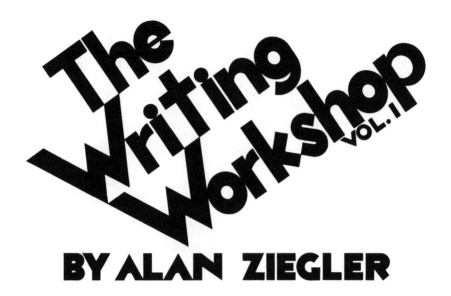

BY ALAN ZIEGLER

Teachers & Writers Collaborative
5 Union Square West, New York, N.Y. 10003

This book is made possible by a grant from the National Endowment for the Arts in Washington, D.C., a federal agency.

Eighth printing

Library of Congress Cataloging in Publication Data

Ziegler, Alan.
  The writing workshop.

  Bibliography: p. 142.
  1. English language—Rhetoric—Study and teaching. 2. Creative writing—Study and teaching. 3. English language—Composition and exercises—Study and teaching.
I. Title.
PE1404.Z5   808'.042'07073   81-16741
ISBN 0-915924-11-0 (v. 1)   AACR2

For
Nancy Larson Shapiro,
who suggested this book and, when that wasn't enough, encouraged it
And for
Betty Levinson, Marilyn Robbins, and Steven Schrader

ACKNOWLEDGMENTS

Brief portions of this book originally appeared, in a different form, in *Journal of a Living Experiment*, *Teachers & Writers Magazine*, and *The Whole Word Catalogue 2* (all published by Teachers & Writers Collaborative).

Selections of student writing in this book come from the following places where I have taught workshops: P.S. 11 (Brooklyn), P.S. 75 (Manhattan), P.S. 173 (Manhattan), P.S. 191 (Manhattan), Wagner Junior High School (Manhattan), Lynbrook High School and West End School (Lynbrook), Finkelstein Memorial Library (Spring Valley), and the Museum of Migrating People (the Bronx).

The fact that the editor's name is generally not included in a book is an injustice I will not perpetuate. Cheryl Trobiani has made the author/editor relationship truly a collaborative one, and I appreciate and admire her contributions to this book.

Others who have commented on the manuscript-in-progress include Lucie Brock-Broido, Marilyn Robbins, and Nancy Larson Shapiro. I thank them.

I would also like to thank:

My associates, past and present, at Teachers & Writers Collaborative—particularly Harry Greenberg, Phillip Lopate, Sue Willis, and Bill Zavatsky—for their contributions to my thinking and sustenance to my spirit.

The administrators, teachers, and students who have welcomed me into their schools, notably in the Lynbrook School District, P.S. 173 (Manhattan), and P.S. 75 (Manhattan).

My writing teachers—Michael Goldman, David Ignatow, Joel Oppenheimer, and Kurt Vonnegut—some of whose ideas have become part of my own teaching and this book.

Bruce Cronnell of the Southwest Regional Laboratory (Los Alamitos, California) for providing me with their Technical Notes examining recent research in the teaching of writing.

PREFACE

The Writing Workshop is primarily concerned with the teaching of creative writing at any grade level, although some ideas may not be applicable with very young students. The "you" referred to throughout the book is the classroom teacher, but an aspiring writer can adapt the material for a self-taught program, or a small group of writers can form a workshop, utilizing the ideas the book presents. Although I deal mostly with the writing of free verse poetry and short "expressive" prose, much of this material can be applied to *any* writing, including essays.

This book is divided into two volumes that combine theory and process with practice and procedure. *Volume One* discusses how to turn the classroom into a writing workshop, the writing process, and the teacher's relationship with student writers. *Volume Two* focuses on how to generate writing via assignments and other means. The two volumes constitute a teaching strategy that emphasizes the individual student.

I have attempted to avoid theory bereft of practical application. The discussions of the teaching process should help you establish an atmosphere conducive to writing in which you can offer assistance to your students; the discussions of the writing process contain information you can share with your students to help them get a palpable sense of what being a writer involves. I have presented more material than could be used in any *one* teaching situation. Pick and choose what is appropriate for your needs.

The Writing Workshop is a sort of "survey course" in writing and the teaching of writing—I have touched on many bases without camping too long on any of them. Because writing cannot be divided into neat, self-contained categories, organizing this book was difficult. Some overlapping ideas are restricted to one section, while others are repeated briefly.

If you consider this to be a "recipe" book for teaching writing, then the most important ingredient is *you*—how you amplify and apply the material and how you relate to your students.

Contents

1

Introduction

Getting started is often the most difficult step in writing. (There, I finally found a way to begin this book.)

To keep going runs a close second.

Well, I'll just pretend we're all sitting around my living room sipping coffee, and someone has asked me to talk about the teaching of writing. I'll lean forward and start speaking—casually. But my guests will have to forgive me if I pause and stare into space for varying intervals, if I rephrase what I am saying until I say it the best way, if I take back something I said an hour before or add something to it, and if I abruptly leave the room for several minutes (or days) at a time.

Although I want this book to sound as if I were talking informally to you (and some of the material derives from things I have said spontaneously in student and in teacher workshops), the distance to the written page is longer than arm's-length. Which is why we need writing workshops.

Although I am by profession a writer and a teacher of writing, I had to learn to write this book as I went along, for one never stops being a student of writing. Learning to write is an ongoing journey, along a portion of which we can accompany our students. My major objectives as a teacher are for students to develop positive attitudes toward writing and to increase their ability to negotiate the entire writing terrain, from conception to completion. I want to leave them better prepared to continue their journeys alone. Sometimes the traveling gets rough.

There is a crisis in writing skills not only among schoolchildren but also among college students and adults. An editor recently remarked to me how shocked she was at the poor quality of writing she gets from *professional* writers. The causes for this crisis have been discussed extensively. You can blame television or the educational system. You can pin the rap on parents or on the perpetual deterioration of "young people today." You can also pin the tail on the donkey, but then you have to do something about it. A supportive yet challenging creative writing workshop—as a staple part of the curriculum and not merely an occasional frill—can help students learn to write clearly and vibrantly.

Writing is a medium that can be used as an art form or for functional purposes (reports, essays, correspondence). Creative writing (which has been known to travel under the aliases "expressive writing" and "imaginative writing") is difficult to define in a way that differentiates it from transactional (or functional) writing. Perhaps this is because different kinds of writing are not that different. I have written in virtually every mode, and my writing process does not vary substantially whether I am writing a poem, article, short story, song, or memo.

The distinctions between creative and transactional writing have more to do with content than with language skills. Transactional writing tends to call for a greater fidelity to objective truth than does creative writing. A journalist writing about a fist fight between two diplomats in a posh restaurant would have to interview the participants and observers to find out what happened and why, while a short-story writer could combine objective facts with unsubstantiated rumor and fancy to fictionalize an account. Likewise, a student writing an essay in response to the proverbial assignment "How I Spent My Summer Vacation" is bound by the constraint of factual accuracy, while a poem or story *based* on the student's summer vacation can be a horse of any color the author chooses.

A poet is more likely than an essayist to assume a persona that is at odds with his or her personality and experience. "The thing I like most about creative writing," a high school student told me, "is that you can be yourself." I replied that you certainly *can* be yourself, but that one of the great appeals of creative writing is that you don't *have* to be yourself. You can "be" someone else or you can speak from a part of yourself that represents the "minority view."

One possible distinction between creative and transactional writing is that in transactional writing the objective (to explain the causes of the Civil War or to convince the reader that solar energy is a good thing) may often be clearer at the outset than the objective for a poem or story (which is sometimes no more than to explore a sliver of an idea or mood or simply to sit down and write). With creative writing, there doesn't need to be a *reason* to write; writing itself can be reason enough.

The common denominator is that any kind of writing involves discovering exactly what you want to say and the best way to say it. There are no literary devices employed in poems and stories that are inappropriate for essays; such "creative" techniques as the use of imagery, metaphor, and vignettes can bring life to an essay. On the other hand, a good essayist's ability to write clearly and convincingly is not contradictory to the makeup of a creative writer.

Conceiving and communicating a series of ideas can be as satisfying a writing experience as getting in touch with and expressing feelings. Therefore, although I emphasize creative writing—in my workshops and in this book—I run a free-form "equal-opportunity" workshop in which no modes of writing are discriminated against. Students can move freely among poetry, fiction, plays, and nonfiction.

I use the phrase "*creative* writing" with the understanding that it may be redundant.

I sometimes ask a new group of writing students to make sounds that express how they feel about being in a writing workshop. "Be honest," I coax. Their responses usually include such noises as "ugh" and "yech." It's a start. I ask the class to translate these guttural sounds into spoken words, then into writing—a quick journey through the evolution of language. One high school student wrote, "When I hear I have to write for school an anger builds up in me," and she traced her anger to frustration: "My mind is like a vault containing scattered thoughts waiting to break out but just can't. Time passes and I just stare at the blank sheet of paper, hoping a sudden splurge will occur and my writer's hand will write away." Even when the "splurge" occurs, as another student pointed out, there are still problems: "It usually comes out like a mess."

Our task as writing teachers is to help students open those "vaults," then to grasp and shape that "splurge" so that even if it does come out like a mess, it doesn't end up as one.

After exploring negative attitudes with new students, I ask "Why bother; what's in it for *you*?" If I receive or can cultivate positive answers to that question, I've laid a foundation for teaching writing. Some students start with a utilitarian response, "Look, I don't enjoy writing but I see how it's necessary." Others see that there's more: "Through writing I can express myself." True, but writing is not only self-expression; it is also self-formation and re-formation. Writing can be an investigatory process that helps us develop a sense of who we are and how we fit into the world of people, places, and ideas. "What do I think and feel?" may be a better way of approaching writing than "This is how I think and feel." Another of the allures of writing was expressed by the student who remarked, "I just like to make things up, tell stories."

My own growth as a writer accelerated when I found out what was in it for me. I wasn't a "born writer." As a child I didn't sit under a tree and copiously fill notebooks with my innermost thoughts; my mind wasn't bursting at the seams with visions that just *had* to be set down on paper. In school I wasn't a naturally graceful writer. But writing was useful, so I worked at it, and as my writing improved, so did my grades. Then it went beyond grades. I began to get hooked when I wrote a review of an Off-Broadway show for the school paper and later found out that a stranger had actually gone to see the show as a result of what I had written. My words could affect what someone did on a Saturday night. (Eighteen years later, that show, "The Fantastiks," is still running, and I am still writing.)

Even so, it wasn't until I started writing poems and stories and discovered that writing could be its own reward—personally meaningful, even *fun* at times—that my writing really took off. Everything improved: sentence structure, grammar, word usage, organization. The most pleasant discovery was that, like muscles, imagination and emotional capacity develop with use. The more I wrote, the more imaginative I became and the more capable of perceiving and articulating emotions. The more I said, the more I had to say. I'm sure this was to some extent an unleashing of dormant qualities, but I think that we all have an artistic capability which can be tapped.

Freud referred to the creative writer as a "strange being" and, speaking for non-writers, declared that "not even the clearest insight into the determinants of the writer's choice of material and into the nature of the art of creating imaginative forms will ever help to make creative writers of *us*." This book, supported by my teaching experiences, is a denial of Freud's statement and his implication that only some people know the secret of being creative writers. Well, if it *is* a secret, then I say, "Pssst...pass it on," with confidence that the secret can be understood by anyone.

Freud has not been the only one to think that creative writers, particularly poets, are *different*. (If this were so, I'd prefer Plato's description of the poet as a "light winged holy creature" to Freud's "strange being.") But creative writers are different from other people only in that they devote more time and energy to expressing themselves with language. A poet is not a special person, just a person who does something special.

Certainly, "talent" is a factor in success as a writer. But no one knows exactly what talent is. No one knows how much of it is natural and how much can be acquired—and even the smallest amount of natural ability can be cultivated. *Wanting* to write enough to try it and persist at it is part of what it takes to write successfully; in fact, "inclination" and "desire" are among the (regrettably) obsolete definitions of talent. The writing teacher should nurture spirit, as well as develop skills.

I tell students that the recipe for making themselves into creative writers

4

might look something like this: Take a pinch of theory and a helping of literary influence, mix with gobs of intuition, marinate with constant practice, and season with feedback.

Many writers have done just fine without ever taking a writing workshop, but how many other people would have derived pleasure and satisfaction from writing if they had been exposed to the guidance of a good teacher? Lord Byron wrote, "Many are the poets who have never penn'd their inspiration." We can reduce that number.

THE TEACHER AS WRITER

When I was first asked to teach a writing workshop, I had no teaching experience. I based those first classes on my own experiences as a writer. Since then, I have learned a great deal about pedagogy, but I still predicate my teaching on what I know about writing. Teachers in whose classes I have worked have told me that an important part of my classroom demeanor is the way I share with students my intimate relationship with language at its most inscrutable, insufferable, and exquisite: the highs of creativity and the lows of drudgery.

I once gave a talk to a group of English teachers interested in improving their students' writing. At lunch, I took a survey of the eight teachers at my table and found that, with the exception of letter writing, all but one of them only wrote when they had to turn out a memo or a newsletter article. Only one teacher also wrote poetry and kept a journal.

I can't overemphasize how important it is for teachers of writing to write themselves. Albert Einstein once said regarding science that "the years of anxious searching in the dark, with their intense longing, their alterations of confidence and exhaustion and the final emergence into the light—only those who have experienced it can understand it." Or, by implication, pass it on to others. Teaching writing, like teaching science, involves more than formulas and procedures. Not that teachers need to experience "years of anxious searching": an occasional hour or so—with emergences into a light of lesser wattage than the likes of Einstein and Shakespeare viewed —can be a great help in teaching.

A school district asked me to teach an in-service course in the Teaching of Creative Writing; at my suggestion the title was changed to A Writing Workshop. I promised the teachers that, at the end, they would not only go back to their classrooms with numerous assignments (everything I'd do with them they could use with their students), but they would also gain a familiarity with the writing process that they could draw on when students had questions or problems.

Talk to your students about your own writing experiences, your problems and techniques for solving them. Share some of your writing, including a piece as it developed from first to last draft. Don't just bring in writing you are confident of, but also bring a piece you are unsure about.

Expose your own vulnerability and ask for reactions. Chances are your students will be gentle with you.

I have read students a couple of poems I wrote when I was in high school and college. They're pretty bad. But I got better, and the contrast between my poems then and now is proof that one can improve.

You can also discuss creative encounters you've had in other fields, particularly as they regard perseverance and problem solving. Poet Gary Snyder has pointed out that a poet can learn a great deal from a master mechanic.

Tolstoy related an anecdote involving the Russian artist Bryulóv: "Once when correcting a pupil's study, Bryulóv just touched it in a few places and the poor dead study immediately became animated. 'Why, you only touched it a *wee bit*, and it is quite another thing!' said one of the pupils. 'Art begins where the *wee bit* begins,' replied Brulyóv, indicating by these words just what is most characteristic of art."

Tolstoy believed that this incident illustrated "what can, and what cannot, be taught in the schools." It is debatable whether art can be "taught," but the more you know about the "wee bit" the better chance you have of trying to teach it.

Perhaps you can form a workshop with interested colleagues in which you can discuss your own writing as well as the teaching of writing. At the secondary school level, it would be a good idea to invite teachers in other disciplines to join or to visit the workshop. Writing teachers can share what they know about the writing process with teachers of such subjects as history and science, who often require their students to write regularly. They, in turn, can talk to the writing teachers about the demands they make on their students to write, so that writing teachers can help prepare students for those tasks.

2

The Writing Workshop

ATMOSPHERE AND ROUTINE

James Tate, a successful poet, spends three hours a day involved with his poetry, which does not mean that he *writes* for three hours a day: "I try to clear my mind to an empty arctic state and wait. . . . I do a lot more thinking about poetry than I do writing it." And if two or three months go by without a single poem being completed, that does not "depress" him. He may then "riffle through fifteen or twenty pages that I have accumulated in the past month, and look for that one starting place."

Well, you might say, that's fine for poets, who don't produce as many words as prose writers, so they can afford to spend more time per word. But listen to what Nicholas Meyer, a popular novelist (*The Seven Percent Solution*), says about his writing habits: "You sit in your little room, drink much coffee and talk to nobody. I have only the dogs to keep me company. I spend a lot of time sitting on the couch, listening to my phonograph and staring at the ceiling."

Now let's turn to a singer/songwriter, Randy Newman, who commented in the middle of a performance, "What am I doing here? I'm a writer. I should be home worrying about not writing." And finally, Pulitzer Prize winning nonfiction writer Annie Dillard said, "I usually get my ideas in November, and I start writing in January. I'm waiting."

So, the writing process has a lot to do with not writing; one does a lot of musing while waiting for the muse. What happens, then, when the words actually start flowing? Vladimir Mayakovsky, the Russian poet, described his experience in this way: "I walk along, waving my arms and mumbling almost wordlessly, now shortening my steps so as not to interrupt my mumbling, now mumbling more rapidly in time with my steps."

Thomas Wolfe wrote standing up, using the top of his refrigerator as a desk. Completed papers would waft to the floor, to be gathered up at the end of each session.

When I teach writing I apply what I know about the writing process, drawing on my own experience and what others have said about how they work. But there are limitations on the extent to which students can model their classroom writing on the work habits of the pros. Envision a teacher's response if the six authors I have mentioned here were in a typical school:

"James, it is the end of the marking period and you have not handed in anything. *Nothing.* You leave me no choice..."

"Nicholas, how many times have I told you that you cannot bring those dogs into this classroom. And shut off that music!"

"Randy, frankly, I'm a little concerned about you. You seem worried all the time."

The teacher, noticing that Annie, like James, has an empty folder, might say, "Annie, dear, I'm waiting." To which Annie would reply, "So am I, ma'am. So am I."

"Thomas, I have warned you about sneaking into the cafeteria kitchen and making a mess of the place."

As for Mayakovsky, he'd be sent right down to the principal's office as a discipline problem: "Vladimir is very disruptive. I think he might be a little disturbed in the head — very hyper, mumbles a lot, can't sit still, makes strange gestures..."

Professionals who desperately want to write often have trouble. Alone at my typewriter, if I take forty-five minutes to position the paper in the roller, no bell sounds ordering me on to another activity, telling me I've blown my opportunity to write for the day. So it may seem like it is asking quite a lot to expect students, many of whom have problems in attitude and/or performance concerning the written word, not only to write, but to write during a prescribed period amid the distractions of a crowded classroom.

And yet, given the proper classroom environment, most students write more and better in class than they do if assigned to write at home. This is partly due to the fact that they have not developed ways and means of writing on their own. The writing process can be so elusive and unreliable that even professional writers, as we have just seen, often have to muster a great deal of self-motivation and willpower to devote long periods of time for small outputs of work. Teachers can actually *use* the time-and-space parameters of the classroom to structure students' writing activities within a group environment conducive to individualized writing (while encouraging students to write at home). The classroom will never be an ideal place for people to write, but we can go as far as possible in that direction.

Exactly how to best transform your classroom into a writing workshop varies from classroom to classroom, depending on, among other things, the age of your students and the amount of time you can devote to writing. The workshop should have a set schedule. I recommend at least one hour twice a week, but high school English teachers might be limited to forty-five minutes once a week, due to class schedules and curriculum pressures.

A writing workshop is a "state of minds," with an atmosphere that supports all aspects of writing, not just putting words down on paper. The workshop, like the weather, varies. Its activities—all of which are regularly pursued by most professional writers but are often missing from the classroom—include:

1. Generating, developing, and revising material
2. Receiving and giving criticism
3. Discussing the writing process
4. Sharing and attempting to solve problems
5. Creating public products, such as publications
6. Time to pause.

A writing workshop, like a basement workshop, is a place for puttering about, as well as for constructing and fixing things.

While the workshop is in session, students should be engaged in some activity related to writing, including such peripheral activities as copying over old work or reading a classmate's poem. At any given time, a visitor might see one or more of the following:

1. An animated discussion about a writing topic
2. A small group offering each other suggestions
3. Some students pouring out words as if their pens had spouts, while others wait for the next line, their knuckles white from clutching suddenly clogged pens
4. Students doing illustrations for a literary magazine
5. Students reading through their folders and notebooks in search of something they'd forgotten they had started
6. A discussion about an exemplary poem, with the emphasis not on what the poem means but rather on what the writer has accomplished and how he/she has done so.

I try to make the workshop as hospitable as possible. As long as students are not disruptive, I accommodate individual work habits. This may involve rearranging the seating when students are writing, allowing some students to cluster in small groups while others go off by themselves. I've let students curl up in corners and perch atop radiators (it's sometimes the closest they can get to a window). There are more than enough stumbling blocks to good writing; discomfort should not be one of them. If the writing gets done, and students respect each other's workspace, I am flexible as to *where* they write.

And, *how* they write. Sometimes elementary school teachers make guidelines for how students should write. Since tools can be as important to writers as they are to carpenters, I allow students to write in whatever ways they find comfortable—with pen or pencil, in print or script, in a notebook or on composition paper. As one who is always on the lookout for the perfect pen and notebook, I know how writers can be finicky about these things. Rudyard Kipling wrote about his loving and demanding relationship with pens, "And with what tools did I work...? I had always been choice, not to say coquettish in this respect....I used a slim, octagonal-sided, agate penholder with a Waverley nib.... when in an evil hour it snapped I was much disturbed. Then followed a procession of impersonal hirelings...which promised well but did not perform." One student indicated his appreciation for being able to use a pen: "I like writing with a pen the most because it feels like the pen is gliding; it makes me go faster than a pencil. When I wrote a letter to my mother I wrote it because I miss her. And I wrote it in pen."

Do not lock the workshop into a tight routine, even if that routine has the best intentions. One teacher told me that she assigns her class a different topic each day, Monday through Thursday; on Friday, each student selects one paper to revise from among the week's work. This way, students are constantly writing, and have freedom of choice over what to revise.

But what happens if Monday's assignment gets a student so excited that he/she wants to revise it on Tuesday, rather than wait until Friday, when it might be stale? Or what if an assignment from three weeks ago suddenly blossoms in a writer's mind, and he/she realizes its rich potential and wants to have another go at it? Or what if Monday's assignment turns into a long work that can be continued throughout the week? All of these variations should be permissible. The writing workshop is not amenable to inflexible organization; students should perceive structure as a friendly aid that can be bypassed when there is a better course available. In my early teaching days a student complained, "It seems there's always something else on my mind more important than the assignment." Now, for the most part, I encourage students to be grateful for and pursue any self-motivation and direction.

I often start a session with discussion of a topic, including, when possible, related samples of writing by professionals and students. The workshop members may then:

—Work on the topic-of-the-day (I've had the whimsical notion of listing the "topic du jour" on a little blackboard, restaurant-style).

—Continue a work-in-progress.

—Revise old work.

—Start something on their own.

Basically, I'm there to help students write, not to impede them. In opening up one possiblity, via an assignment, my intention is not to close off other possibilities. When asked to evaluate my workshop at the end of a term, many students have commented on how important it was for them to be able to follow the beats of their own drummers, while they were also grateful for the ideas I gave them. I make it clear to the class that in the long run it will be helpful for them to try as many of my assignments as possible, because the assignments are designed to give them a wide range of writing experiences, many of which they might not otherwise discover on their own. But I am not usually concerned about *when* they do the assignments.

This multi-option approach takes some time to evolve. Early in a workshop term I strongly encourage everyone to do the same assignment, because I want students to have a backlog of common writing experiences that can serve as reference points throughout the term. Also, I want to establish my leadership with the group. When I feel respected by the students, I am then strong enough to stand back and let things happen, knowing I can pull everyone together when it's appropriate, such as when I am exploring new literary territory or when either behavioral or literary discipline breaks down.

For me, a workshop is going well when the room is filled with involved students. When you veer away from a highly structured routine, the classroom may occasionally get too disorderly. Students can abuse freedom, especially when they don't know quite what to do with it, and there are times when the buzzing around the room has little to do with creative writing. Lack of focus can result from frustration or laziness, and when that happens you should take stock of what is going on. I find that a class collaboration or a mandatory assignment may then get the class back into a working frame of mind.

Once a workshop is off and running, you should feel like you can, on any given day, give a structured assignment, turn the students loose to work on their own, or simply take the time to *talk* with the class about writing or anything else that's on their minds. Don't be surprised if many students come up with material for writing out of these enjoyable but seemingly aimless conversations.

Each teacher will shape the workshop to his / her own style. I can only guarantee one thing: No matter how much you accomplish, no matter how much gets written, when it is over you will realize how much you *haven't* done — the projects that were talked about but didn't materialize, the assignments you never got around to using. A colleague, novelist Richard Perry, once overheard me complaining about how much I wanted to cram into the waning weeks of a workshop. Walking by without stopping, he laughed and said, "There is *never* enough time." Obvious, right? Simply stated? But those words keep reverberating in my mind, like a line from a great poem.

What follows is a look at some aspects of a writing workshop.

EQUIPMENT

The Folder. The workshop revolves around the students' folders, in which they keep everything they write, including all drafts, notes, and fragments. To avoid confusion, students can mark their drafts "D" and final versions "F" (sometimes an "F" is subsequently changed to a "D"). Requiring that everything be retained puts the emphasis on process rather than product, and students feel a sense of accomplishment as their folders get thicker.

Students can periodically go through their folders and try to develop notes and fragments or work on revision. Sometimes leftovers from dinner come in handy, and so it goes with writing; that story you couldn't quite pull together in October may be tackled with renewed appetite in November, and the fragment you had no time for in December can be quite appealing during a famine in January. Unsuccessful pieces can, in a kind of alchemical procedure, be made precious, with the intervention of time and a steadily growing acquaintance with the craft of writing.

I encourage students to decorate their folders in any way they see fit, suggesting they do it in small doses — little drawings, grafitti, notes, doodles. Often, the folder becomes a visual correlative to the workshop, and by the end of the term looks quite lived in. Many writers find that a diversionary activity such as doodling provides a good micro-vacation from writing.

One option for students when writing and rewriting seem like mountains too steep to climb is to make neat copies of previously finished work. This is a satisfying endeavor, and students often make textual improvements in the process. They can clip the neat copies together in the front of the folders. These copies are useful when someone wants to read what they have been writing, and when a publication or reading is being organized.

Lost folders are preventable tragedies; I do not allow students to take them home. I generally let a single work-in-progress be taken home, but suggest that the student first make a copy to leave in the folder.

The Notebook. Each student should have a portable notebook, which is his/her personal property and can be taken home. While I am always glad to look at any or all entries, students are never required to hand in their notebooks. For some students, having a notebook that is not critically evaluated unlocks a flood of writing. Perhaps they feel a sense of freedom in knowing that no one will see what they write unless they choose to release it into the world, or perhaps it's merely the feeling of accomplishment that comes from filling all those tiny pages. A more important factor is that one gets to feel *comfortable* with a notebook once it has been broken in. Some students hardly ever touch their notebooks, but there are also many professional writers who don't utilize them.

The writer's notebook can encompass the function of a diary, but it is also a personal writing workshop where poems and stories often bud. The notebook is a "halfway house" for notes and fragments that can get deposited anytime, anywhere, until they are plucked out and find a permanent home in a piece of writing (although for many words, the notebook is their final resting place). So much of what we think, feel, and observe slips away from us, like air seeping out of a tire. The notebook not only plugs that leak by being a place to talk to ourselves without forgetting what we have said, but the very act of recording our thoughts and observations tends to stimulate mental and verbal sharpness.

I find it is useful to have two notebooks—a full-sized one that I use at home and to travel with, and a small one that I carry around with me. (A couple of index cards makes a good alternative to carrying a notebook around.) In my pre-notebook days, I lost many ideas and flashes of inspiration because I had no place to hold them for safekeeping. Poet David Ignatow has kept a journal throughout his adult life, and this entry demonstrates why it is important for a writer also to have a portable notebook: "This morning I had an insight into love and self-centeredness, as I walked the street on an errand, and now I can't recall it, pressed by duties at home."

Writers can become obsessive in using their notebooks, like photographers who can't pass up anything that remotely looks like an interesting picture. In his early short story "The Notebook," Norman Mailer deftly describes one of the pitfalls of being so anxious to preserve events for posterity that one cannot live them fully. The narrator is having an argument with his girlfriend and succumbs to the need to write about the argument in his notebook while it is still taking place:

> *Emotional situation deepened by notebook,* he wrote. *Young writer, girlfriend. Writer accused of being observer, not participant in life by girl. Gets idea he must put in notebook. Does so, and brings the quarrel to a head. Girl breaks relationship over this.*
> "You have an idea now," the young lady murmured.
> "Mmm," he answered.
> "That notebook. I knew you'd pull out that notebook." She began to cry.
> "Why, you're nothing but a notebook," . . . .

This will not be a danger for most students, for whom writing things down outside of school is not as common as reaching for the television dial. I considered it a victory when a teacher told me that her class, with whom I'd been working, had been on a field trip when the subway broke down between stations. "Half of them pulled out their notebooks and wrote down people's reactions," she said.

If our budget allows, I buy students little notebooks; otherwise I encourage them to buy notebooks themselves. I read my classes excerpts from the published notebooks of famous writers and then ask them to use their own notebooks however they see fit for a while before we discuss it further. After a couple of weeks, I ask what they have been writing about in their notebooks, and I list the responses on the board. This approach allows students to make their own discoveries and share them with each other. Here's a typical list of notebook topics given by my students:

— Happenings
— Dreams
— Memories
— Nature
— Places
— Thoughts
— Images
— World Situations
— About Writing
— People's Behavior
— Hopes
— Reactions
— Overheard Conversations

The major characteristic of a writer's notebook is that *anything* can be included, in any form. Nothing need be finished or refined. Entries can be as short as one word which the student wants to look up in the dictionary or possibly use in a poem. When writing in their notebooks, students should have a sense of total freedom.

As the notebook fills, it becomes a treasure chest of potential literary material. The French writer Max Jacob lamented the fact that he had not kept extensive notebooks: "If I had written the journal of my life from day to day I should now have the Larousse dictionary. You hear a word, you collect it, and there you have the reconstitution of a whole atmosphere. Oh, all the things you lose! All those lost pearls! Write the journal of your life."

David Ignatow has often been able to use the raw material in his notebooks: "I would sit down at night and tell myself the immediate thoughts that were going through my mind, to perhaps gradually evolve from these thoughts an image or a metaphor that would sum up the whole thing. It would often be the beginning of a poem." Even if students don't subsequently use the material in their notebooks, the process of listening, observing, contemplating, and notating will advance their growth as writers.

These are brief excerpts from typical student notebooks:

Climbing the mountain upstate Kingston

addidas, puma

"Hello what is your name?"

My parents are separated. Last night my father came to help me with my math. But he wasn't up to it. The next day I thought maybe my father had slept over. I was right.

Words from nowhere: I don't got to do what you want me to
I don't got ta

14

These excerpts are from the notebooks of sixth-grader Isabel Feliz:

> It's not as if I'm a shy and lonely girl trying to find herself, or a rich person trying to be popular. Nothing of the sort. At times I just feel left out because everybody else has somebody to stick with. . . .

> Maybe sometimes I feel strange about being alive — being able to talk, move, hear, and see. . . .

> When a friend asks you, for example, "Do you like that hat?" you ask, "Do *you*?". . . . There's a fear of ridicule. . . .

> . . . When I got home and told my mother she seemed all of a sudden so excited. I don't know why. To me, winning a contest with three other people seemed nothing to get so excited about. I would have probably been more excited *if I* had won alone. No, but that would have been selfish. I would have probably been more scared & nervous also, if I had won alone.

> When you write, you're not only making up the story but you're living through it.

> The whole class is talking and playing. Once in a while someone comes and asks, "What are you doing, Isy?" I just nod and keep on writing.

> I lay down my pen, close this book and REST!

TWO RULES

An indispensable rule for my writing workshops, which I carefully state at the outset, is: *Any piece of writing can be totally factual, totally made-up, or anywhere in between, AND IT IS NOBODY'S BUSINESS WHICH IT IS.*
Writers vary as to how much of their personal lives they reveal in their work. Some writers draw heavily on their experiences and emotions, and they expose to strangers the kinds of intimacies other people share only with those closest to them, if at all. Other writers almost always invent what they write or utilize other people's experiences. Most writers fluctuate between these extremes.
No matter how "autobiographical" a work is, it has passed through an artistic "filter" which probably has made subtle alterations in the raw material. The writer, like the actor, is always wearing a mask, even when the mask bears close resemblance to the writer's self.
Thomas Wolfe used his own life extensively in his novels. In the preface to *Look Homeward, Angel* Wolfe commented that he had "written of experience. . . which was once part of the fabric of [my] life." But, he cautioned, "fiction is not fact, but fiction is fact selected and understood, fiction is fact arranged and charged with purpose," and "a novelist may turn over half the people in a town to make a single figure in his novel." In an author's note for her book *Black Tickets* Jayne Ann Phillips wrote that

"characters and voices in these stories began in what is real, but became, in fact, dreams." On the other hand, authors who write about "invented" situations can also reveal things about themselves—by what they choose to invent. Wolfe noted that "a more autobiographical work than *Gulliver's Travels* cannot easily be imagined."

Students sometimes hold back in their writing. There may be facts about themselves they are hesitant to expose; or they may be afraid that something they make up will be taken as factual or be analyzed as expressing the way they *really* feel "deep inside." Students may be wary of classmates' reactions—which can include teasing as well as sincere but unwanted understanding—or may worry about what the teacher will think.

There is no getting around the fact that writers reveal *something* whenever they write. Any classroom questioning or analysis regarding what might be revealed can inhibit students, however, and make them overly cautious about what they write. Some caution is probably a good idea—with the amount varying for each individual—but the following classroom guidelines can make it easier for students to write openly.

Students should be told never to assume that anything classmates write has really happened or is the way they truly feel. Even if they recognize some aspects as factual, they should understand that the situation might have been altered during the creative process. For example, a student might write about divorced parents who hit each other; while it may be a fact that the parents are divorced, it does not necessarily follow that they hit each other.

Because this is a creative writing workshop and not a therapy group or gossip session, it is off limits to ask questions like "Did that really happen?" or "Do you really feel that way?" or to make comments like "You're *weird*!" (or *sad* or *perverted*, etc.). If someone outside the workshop asks a question they don't wish to answer, students can smile mysteriously and say something deliciously insufferable, like "I'm sorry, but I don't discuss my work."

I don't want people to relate to me on the basis of everything that goes on in my writing. I generally try to extend that same "separation of poem and person" to my students; but there are times when my relationship with a student transcends literary issues, and I do not overlook the connection between the written work and the writer. If I decide to react to a piece as anything other than a literary work, however, I do it privately. And I do it with great care.

The second rule I have is far simpler to deal with: *Students should not throw out anything they have written.* Not only might a student find all or part of an unsuccessful piece salvageable in the future, but something the student thinks is inferior might be better than he/she realizes. Writers often can't distinguish their jewels from their garbage. I once saw a student dropping shreds of what had once been a poem into a garbage can, and we had the following conversation:

ALAN: Why did you do that?
STUDENT: It wasn't any good.
ALAN: That's pretty arrogant. Who told you that you were so smart?
STUDENT: I didn't say I was so smart. In fact I said it wasn't any good.
ALAN: Well, did it ever occur to you that you might not be smart enough as a critic to tell how good you are as a writer or that you might not be able to recognize all the possibilities?

This rule is not inflexible. Sometimes it is difficult for a student to resist the temptation to crumple a piece of paper that has refused to cooperate. But it is good for them to retain as much work as possible so they don't feel that any of their efforts are "waste."

PROGRESS

It is not always easy to gauge how much progress is being made in a workshop. Sometimes there appears to be little growth: the students are listless; the writing is lightweight; the discussions are pallid. But suddenly things come together, and you reap the cumulative effect of what has gone before. I once taught a seminar of five high school students, which met in a conference room. It was an ideal situation—a small group of volunteers in an intimate setting. Yet although I talked and talked, I got little writing in return. At times I felt as if they were all in the ocean, content to tread water; they weren't sinking, but they weren't getting anywhere either. I was discouraged.

One morning I decided I couldn't listen to another of my own monologues, so I brought in a tape of some jazz piano. I shut off the overhead light, leaving on a small desk lamp. "Write anything you want," I said, hopefully but not optimistically. I closed my eyes and thought about a job I used to have transporting boxes. It was so simple: I took boxes from one place and put them in another. The boxes had no choice.

I slowly became aware that something was happening in the dimly lit room. Four of the students were writing steadily, pausing occasionally to listen to the music. The other one, a filmmaker, just listened; but he explained later that he had been "watching" a film develop behind his eyelids. Although it might have appeared that he was the only one not working, he was creating.

The bell rang. Time for lunch. Usually they would have been milling around the doorway for several minutes by now. This time they were still writing and said: "Can we keep going?" "Wow, I wrote a lot." "Those things I wrote—I never knew they were in my head before." "I forgot we were sitting here. I really feel good today." The filmmaker started describing his film.

The poems were good, reflecting ideas I had been talking to them about. An observer at that session would have thought that teaching writing was almost effortless; but what occurred in that session was really the payoff for a great deal of previous effort. The music was a factor, but it would not have had the same effect a few sessions earlier. The time was right for a harvest.

I'm not saying that you should never get discouraged—there's no way to avoid that. I'm saying you may be blessedly lifted out of your discouragement when you least expect it. (Also, discouragement can sometimes fuel new teaching approaches by getting you to try something different.) It's the same with writing. Sometimes it is going nowhere; false starts (if there are any starts at all) and dead ends abound. Then it all comes together. It won't sustain itself for long at that level, but it is wonderful while it lasts.

The progress of individual students can also be difficult to measure, partly because a student whose output is low may be stockpiling input. The following poem by third-grader Omar Smart utilizes good observation and linebreak skills, the kind that might be used by an experienced author:

Once when my aunt died in
California you should see the
ambulance with the sirens
going around Rooo Rooo Rooo Rooo
it was skinning
blocks
My mother
looked out the window
we ran down the
stairs my aunt was
lying on the ground
Isha said what
are you lying on the
ground for
it's dirty
They picked her up
and put her in the
ambulance.

This was Omar's first poem in the workshop—written after several sessions of apparent nonparticipation. I had been tempted to ask the teacher to find another activity for him while I was with the class, but I'm glad I didn't because Omar went on to become an enthusiastic participant in the writing workshop.

Whit Burnett taught fiction writing at Columbia University. His wife Hallie (with whom he edited *Story* magazine) has described his experience with a "dark-eyed, thoughtful young man who sat through one semester of a class in writing without taking notes, seemingly not listening, looking out the window. A week or so before the semester ended, he suddenly came to life. He began to write. Several stories seemed to come from his typewriter at once, and most of these were published. That young man was J. D. Salinger, apparently indulging in 'purposeful reverie,' that courting period of which Somerset Maugham wrote."

RISKS

Writing pieces that just don't "make it" indicates effort, and I value risk taking and overreaching — both in style and subject matter — more than I value safe but lifeless writing. "Take chances," I tell students, "it's foolish to stick with the foolproof. To become a good writer you must risk doing some bad writing." A student once commented that when writing is at its best, "you get into it so much your hand is like a skater on ice." But every skater stumbles occasionally and winds up sitting on the ice. Students should perceive the writing workshop as being big enough for room to "fall." It's a good thing that babies don't understand the concept of "clumsiness," or else they'd never learn to walk. Any aspiring dancer, athlete, or painter must likewise risk awkwardness and failure. The biggest mistake students can make is to be so afraid of mistakes that they stunt their own growth.

PROBLEMS

Plagiarism. Plagiarism (alias "copying") is a sensitive issue which should be discussed with students near the beginning of the term. I also bring it up again briefly before material is submitted to the literary magazine, lest any student suffer the embarrassment of having a plagiarized piece published. I point out to the class that one of the motives for plagiarism is the need to produce. Just as some people rob as a result of poverty, some people plagiarize because they are unable to support their creative selves. Like robbery, plagiarism is against the law.

A good fifth-grade writer I'll call Susan once handed in a clever poem about children at the beach. The poem rhymed, which was unlike Susan's writing or that of any of the others in the class. My first reaction was, "Good, we'll have a token rhymer for the literary magazine." But as I looked carefully at the poem I realized it didn't have Susan's voice—it was the kind of poem written *for*, not *by* children. I discussed this with Susan, and she admitted copying the poem from a book. "Why?" I wanted to know, "you're such a good writer, and your own poems are so much more natural." She replied that she'd copied the poem *because* she had been so prolific and successful and didn't know how to deal with not having something new to hand in. She didn't want to disappoint me. I told her that although I was glad she was interested in pleasing me with her writing, pleasing herself should be more important: "You can't please yourself by saying you wrote something you didn't write." I would say essentially the same thing to any student who plagiarized out of insecurity that he/she was not a good writer, and I would add that the best way to improve is by persevering.

There are occasions, with younger children, when one child will accuse another of writing "the same thing!" and the other will often reply, "I wrote it first!'' All you can do in this situation is arbitrate. If it is impossible for you to determine who is copying from whom or if there has been a mutual transfer of words, you can suggest that they turn the work into a collaboration. You can point out that in the future, when they look over someone's shoulder and see something they are tempted to copy, they could say, "Hey, that's a great idea, can we work on it together?" or, "Can I use it if I give you credit?"

A related situation occurs when a student brings in a piece of writing that a parent or older sibling has "helped" with to such an extent that it is markedly different from what the student has been writing. I encourage students to work with members of their families, but tell them that they should give co-authorship credit when appropriate. (If they do not want a parent to become *too* involved in the writing of a piece, they should make it clear that while they appreciate any help and suggestions they want to make the final decisions themselves.)

Students should not feel pressured to produce new work constantly. Workshop options — including revising, making neat copies of finished pieces, and collaborating—plus an awareness that writing ideas often don't come right away during any given session should reduce the likelihood of the desperation that breeds plagiarism.

Sometimes students don't copy words but use ideas they've gotten from other sources, such as plots from books, television shows, movies, and comics. If a student writes something similar to another work, you can suggest they adapt it into another medium: short stories or parts of novels can be put into play form, and material from television and movies can be written as prose. Adaptation is a legitimate form of writing as long as it is done aboveboard, with proper credit to the original source. (One of the motion picture Oscar categories is for a screenplay based on work from another medium, usually a novel.)

Several of my classes have been fascinated with the legal aspects of plagiarism. Creative work is property, and you can't take a story that belongs to someone else any more than you can take another's car. Students will ask, "But what if it's just a *coincidence* that you thought of the same thing someone else did?" or "What happens if you don't steal on purpose —you read something a long time ago but you forgot about it, so you think you're making it up?" Tricky questions like these get resolved in the courtroom. The most important point in the classroom is for students to realize that even if they get away with it the rewards for stealing someone else's work are empty. Any praise they would receive, while perhaps initially pleasing, would likely become a haunting echo.

Competition and Revenge. Competition is unavoidable. Some students will fret over whether they are "better" or "worse" writers than their classmates. This can actually be a motivating factor, prodding Johnny to work harder so he can get the kind of compliments being showered on

Susan. Students can also become motivated by a classmate's negative criticism of their work—a kind of "I'll show *you!*" attitude. In this case, writing well is the best revenge.

Although I don't encourage these attitudes, I don't demand purity of spirit either. Some of my best friends, and I, have at times been motivated by competition and a desire for revenge. But when I sense that such factors are inhibiting rather than stimulating a young writer, I will say something. If Johnny gives up because he thinks he can't write like Susan or because someone told him his writing "stinks," I will point out that writers should not be intimidated into inactivity by what others write or say. I myself have been jealous of writers who could do things with language that I couldn't, only to find out eventually that the feeling was *mutual.* And for a writer to let criticism stop him / her from progressing is one way of assuring that a criticism will remain true (if, indeed, it was true to begin with).

Silence. Most of us fear silence in the classroom during a discussion almost as much as a TV talk-show host dreads "dead air." But not all silence is dead; sometimes it is a necessary part of the life of the workshop, especially when problem solving is going on.

Once I was discussing "Changes" with a sixth-grade class. The students talked excitedly about the way things change, but when I asked, "How would you apply these ideas to a piece of writing?" there was silence. I could have offered several suggestions, but I sensed that it was an appropriate time to give each student the opportunity of a small struggle. Yes, it can be an opportunity to struggle, one we often deprive our students of. In trying to be helpful—to get the reward of hearing "You always come up with such good ideas"—we sometimes don't allow students to make their own discoveries. We deprive them of the joy of grasping something tangible out of a morass of abstraction.

No writing ideas about changes were forthcoming. The silence extended from seconds to minutes. I was changing from being confident and in control of the class to being nervous and apprehensive that no one would speak until the bell rang. I was just about to talk to the class about this change in my nervous system—anything instead of silence—when a hand tentatively went up, then another. There was a snowballing effect and soon the class was rolling again. I exhaled fully for the first time in ten minutes as I filled the board with their suggestions.

Nature hates a vacuum; sometimes we have to shut up and let nature take its course—if we don't fill the vacuum, someone else will. It's a good idea, though, to discuss this with your students so they don't interpret the silence as your inability to lead a discussion.

ACTIVITIES

Reading Out Loud. Reading out loud—pieces by both published writers and students—is a useful workshop activity. Skilled writers usually acquire an "ear" for the music and rhythms of language, the way words sound and work together. Listening carefully to work read out loud can help train students' "writer's ears." You might read a piece several times, asking students to concentrate once or twice on the content, and then on the sounds (or vice versa, although that's more difficult). Occasionally, as a piece is read out loud, ask a couple of students to "graph" it on the board, like a cardiogram, reflecting the rhythm and levels of intensity. This will get students to listen extra carefully.

After you read a piece of writing out loud, ask the students which words or phrases made them see something, evoked an emotional response, or stuck in their minds for any other reason, including "they sounded good." In order to minimize pressure and maximize participation, emphasize that quotes from heard writings do not have to be verbatim. (In fact, misquotes can be interesting and useful. When misquotes occur, students often find something they can use in their own writing. I myself have often gotten ideas from miss-hearing song lyrics playing in the background.)

This activity helps students not only to develop listening skills but also to become aware of how language is used effectively. At its best, writing has the almost magical effect of evoking images or emotions. See if students can figure out for any given piece the "magic words" that make this "trick" work.

When it's practical, you can mimeograph a text, but I suggest you read the piece out loud *before* distributing copies, because some students don't listen as intently when the words are in front of them. They know they can tune out now and read later, or they follow the words on the page without paying attention to the sounds.

Set aside about 15 minutes occasionally for a student mini-reading. Have volunteers take turns going to the front of the room and reading selections from their work. Sometimes a student will ask a friend to read for him/her. That's all right with me because this is a writing, not a public speaking, workshop. Writers sometimes get a "bursting" feeling when they finish something, and they want to share it immediately. When this happens, I am also open to spontaneous student readings, perhaps of a single piece.

Memorable Words. Ask students to keep a file of memorable lines or phrases from songs, articles, advertisements, posters, and television commercials. Not the whole piece, just a few words or a line or two that have caught the student's eyes or ears. Read a batch of these phrases out loud and see if there is anything to be gleaned regarding their effectiveness: Do they illustrate any points that have been discussed in the workshop, such as use of imagery or poetic license? Or just read them for entertainment and enjoy them with no discussion. If an excerpt suffers from lack of context, you might ask the student to discuss the original piece and how the part selected works in relation to the whole.

Students can also keep a file of excerpts from overheard conversations on the bus, at home, in a store, on the street, in the hallway. Compare these language kernels with the ones from printed sources discussed above. These activities will encourage students to pay more attention to the language they come across in their daily lives.

Ask students to go to the poetry section of the school or public library and select a poem they had not known before and which they react to strongly. The poem can be compelling in any way. The student may love, hate, or be perplexed by it, as long as the poem sticks in his/her mind. Read and discuss the selections, explaining any conflicting reactions as evidence of the fact that responses to poetry can be as varied as approaches toward writing it.

Word Doctors. It is a common practice for movie and play producers to call in a "script doctor" to infuse life into a lame piece of writing. Start a "hospital" for sick pieces of writing: a cardboard box into which anyone, anytime, can place a piece of writing with which they are dissatisfied. The writing may need editing—deletions, rearrangements, etc.—or it may need a complete overhaul. The box's contents are always available to students who wish to act as "word doctors." More than one student can work either independently or cooperatively on the same piece.

"Word doctors" can offer suggestions to the author, or they can take it upon themselves to rewrite (but they should always keep a copy of the original). The result can be a successful collaboration or a dissonant clash of writers' egos ("You made it even *worse*!"). However the work turns out, it can keep the workshop interesting, especially when two students work separately on the same piece and then compare their results.

Inventory. Businesses take inventories in order to get a sense of what's been happening and what should happen. Periodically ask students to rummage through their folders and notebooks and take an inventory of writing ideas, unfinished projects, works that need revision, lines that were never pursued, and strong lines in otherwise weak pieces of writing.

You can contribute to the inventory by asking questions, including: "What haven't you written about that you would like to write about?" "What form have you been meaning to get around to—poem, play, song, story, etc.?" "What kind of response would you like to get from a reader, and how could you go about getting it?"

With student input you can also make a list of the areas the workshop has worked in or discussed and another list of things you and the students would like to get around to. The first list will give the class a sense of perspective, especially if you point out the interrelationships among the items, and the second list will come in handy in the future.

Word-Gifts. Have students give words as gifts. The gift can be a single word ("stellar"), an image ("snow smothering an airplane wing"), advice ("read Judy Blume"), a piece of information ("there's a sale on pens at Murray's stationery store"), a setting ("a wilderness retreat for teenage movie stars"), or a character ("a fifth-grader whose divorced parents are remarrying—each other"). This event could take place on a student's birthday or before Christmas vacation. You can suggest that recipients use their gifts in future writings.

At the end of a series of workshops, students can give each other more personal word-gifts, such as, "I love the poem you wrote about your grandmother" or "You gave a lot of good suggestions." It might be best for students to exchange word-gifts only within small feedback groups (see Group Feedback) so they can give proper consideration to what they give.

Failures. Periodically devote a class to "failures." Students should learn that a failed piece of writing is not a waste of time, because through such experiences we learn about process, discover useful material, and/or eliminate one approach, perhaps paving the way for future success.

Ask several students to select a piece of writing that didn't meet their expectations, and do the same with one of your own. Have each writer discuss the aims of the piece and what might have gone wrong along the way. The other students can make suggestions regarding the specific material of the failed piece or can offer tips for the future.

A baseball player who makes an out seven times out of ten is considered to be quite a good batter, and the same holds for creative writers—one who "writes .300" is doing pretty well. (One student had even lesser expectations: She planned to write three haikus a day for ten years, at the end of which she would have written 10,950 poems, including "about ten or eleven good ones.") The difference between baseball players and writers is that with writing it's harder to tell which pieces are "hits." There's no accounting for tastes—ten editors reject a manuscript and the eleventh loves it. The author may be the last to know he/she has written something wonderful, or awful. I've had poems published that I thought were weak, while ones I felt were "masterpieces" have gone unprinted. One result of the "failure" session might be that students will get positive reactions for pieces they would otherwise have abandoned.

Begin each subsequent class on failures with an update segment, during which students report on the effects of the previous session.

GRADES

Whenever I discuss grading, I feel like I should whisper; creative writers aren't supposed to talk about such things. Everyone knows that a poem or story should not—indeed *cannot*—be graded and that to put an "A" or "B" or "C" on the top of a paper containing a young person's deepest feelings is an act of defacement. I agree, but some form of evaluation is often necessary at the secondary-school level, especially when the writing workshop is part of a graded English class.

Secondary-school students are graded on virtually everything they do. Therefore, in the value system of many students, the absence of a grade may imply that creative writing is not among the "real" goods of their education. Not getting grades for creative writing can have several negative results: cause it to slip to the bottom of a student's priority list, especially when term papers and exams pile up; allow uncooperative students to avoid making an honest effort (which may make it harder for others to work) with no threat of penalty; and, most important, deprive students who work hard at their writing of the reward of a good grade. Also, students who don't do well academically may blossom in the workshop; it's another shot at success for them.

With this stated, I adamantly oppose the grading of individual pieces of writing, recommending instead an overall grade of "Plus," "Pass," or "Minus" based on the student's completed folder (which includes drafts and fragments). A "Plus" adds several points to a student's class average, and a "Minus" subtracts an equal number. I take into account the student's attitude; extra effort might be the difference between a "Pass" and a "Plus," while "Minus" is reserved for students who do not make an honest effort.

It is important to grade students only at the end of the workshop, rather than at intervals, to allow for those who write in streaks — fallow periods alternating with sudden flurries of work. A personal conference during the term can give students a sense of how you feel about what they are doing. Grading individual pieces is a bad idea because it would be impossible at the end of the term to average the grades, and it puts too much emphasis on product rather than process. I wrote a poem for my college freshman English class, and I recall getting quite excited about how everything finally fell into place. Unfortunately, my teacher didn't think highly of the places into which the poem fell, and he gave me a C+, a deflating experience for me. Looking back at the poem, I now agree with his judgment, but I disagree with the manner in which he expressed it.

I participated in a district administrators' meeting to determine how to evaluate their writing program. Someone suggested that the students' folders be evaluated according to the extent the work improved. I, on the other hand, cautioned that growth in writing is not as linear as growth in physical stamina or in the ability to handle mathematical equations. Although there is usually a general *pattern* of improvement, it would not be unusual for the fourth piece of writing to be the best and for the next-to-last piece to be awful. There are days when a writer not only doesn't have "it" but can hardly remember what "it" is.

Evaluation should work both ways. At the end of each term, I ask students to evaluate the workshop—its good and bad points. They should specify what they found particularly helpful as well as anything they didn't feel was useful. In addition, I ask them to discuss one or two writing experiences in order to increase my insight into the writing process.

The Writing Workshop—Postscript

These are excerpts from an advertisement:

CREATION of truly outstanding work...
IMAGINATION to give each...the look & feel & texture of its birth.
UNDERSTANDING of the way...
SYMPATHY to help in any way we can.
WE CAN HELP...because we care.

No, this isn't an advertisement for a writing workshop, but rather for Sam's Dry Cleaning.

3

Inspiration and the Unconscious

Conversation overheard in a high school writing workshop:

"You haven't even started? How long does it take you to think of something?"

"I'm getting inspired."

"I thought I smelled something burning. By the time you do your poem, your autobiography will be dead."

What is inspiration and where does it come from? This is no slouch in the Heavyweight Question category, and if you are taking a deep breath before reading on, you can imagine how I feel before writing on; my deep breath has lasted two months. Much that is said about creativity is either vague, comprehensible but difficult to put into practice, or paradoxical at best and contradictory at worst.

Thinking too much about the unconscious can make you feel like putting your brain into a sling before you think on it again. But a good class discussion on creativity can help students articulate and clarify things they know intuitively and experientially, and it can illuminate new possibilities. It can be beneficial just for students to know that others have had similar thoughts and experiences. Such talk can be fascinating and helpful as long as students realize that there are no definitive answers. I recommend discussing the creative process *after* students have done a lot of writing, so that they can contribute to the discussion. Inspiration—how to get it and what to do with it—is at the heart of the creative process.

The Greeks explained the source of creative inspiration with a myth (as they explained other questions that couldn't be answered): Muses descend from the heavens and inspire poets and artists. Such outside intervention has always been a popular explanation, or metaphor, for inspiration (the derivation of the word is "to breathe in"): Gerard Manley Hopkins credited God, and Rudyard Kipling credited a "Daemon." Inspiration has also been described in terms of transformation to another "place"; poet Robert Bly points out, "In ancient times... the poet flew from one world to another, 'riding on dragons,' as the Chinese said."

Modern psychology emphasizes intervention from *within*: the unconscious is the fountain of inspiration. If the unconscious can create while we dream, it makes sense that it also works for us while we are awake in front of a typewriter or easel. Dreams flow effortlessly without conscious control, so it is plausible that creative expression can be facilitated by opening ourselves to and harnessing our unconscious forces. The surrealist movement was based on this principal.

But what of skill, craft, hard work, and discipline? What is the interrelationship between these factors and unconscious "inspiration"?

C. G. Jung wrote of two modes of literary creation: There are consciously crafted works that "spring wholly from the author's intention to produce a particular result," and there are works that "positively force themselves upon the author; his hand is seized, his pen writes things that his mind contemplates with amazement." These latter works originate in the unconscious, from a "creative urge" that can be thought of as "a living thing implanted in the human psyche."

I don't see creative writing as emanating from either a totally conscious or totally unconscious source. For most people, creativity involves an interplay between control and lack of control, conscious effort and instinct. In virtually all of my writing, the unconscious and conscious dance with each other, taking turns leading. There are instances when I feel bathed by unconscious material, which I must consciously mold into an artistic form. Other times, I start with a conscious plan, and during the composition process unconscious forces come into play.

Poet Robert Hayden described the process by which he composed one of his poems: "I knew there were certain things I wanted to do... but I couldn't be deliberate about everything.... some things I consciously tried to get into the poem, and some elements appeared unexpectedly, rather like spontaneous combustion...."

Although there isn't complete agreement on exactly what the unconscious is, or how it works, we know that it brings about creative outbursts. Gustave Flaubert doubted the literary usefulness of these outbursts, which he called "masked balls of the imagination," from which one emerges "having seen only falsity and uttered nothing but nonsense." I wouldn't go that far; I've gotten some pretty good results from these "balls." But, although spontaneity can produce some exciting and

28

fascinating work, it is usually the case that raw, unconscious "data" must be put through a skillful manipulation, which includes selectivity, ordering, expansion, and condensation.

———

Receptivity is often mentioned as a chief component of the creative process—writers use such words as "listening," "expectant," and "waiting." The unconscious is a warehouse of images, ideas, memories, and emotions, with the ability to make connections among these things and current outside stimuli. One can tap this warehouse by being alert—the artist as sentinel, looking and listening with the mind's eye and ear for an indication that something is coming. Students should be made aware of the need to "listen" for the knock on the door separating the conscious from the unconscious and to open up and become an involved host: Virginia Woolf once conceived a novel while taking a bath, and Albert Einstein said he got ideas while shaving. Students should also be alert for overheard phrases or occurrences across the street that might spark a creative fire in the unconscious.

It is not enough to tell students to "listen and ye shall find." There has to be some seeking, too. Tchaikovsky likened inspiration to a guest who "does not always respond to the first invitation. . . . inspiration will come to those who can master their *disinclination* (to work)." The germ of a composition can come "suddenly and unexpectedly," he said. "If the soil is ready—that is to say, if the disposition for work is there — it takes root with extraordinary force and rapidity, shoots up through the earth, puts forth branches, leaves and, finally, blossoms."

Creative breakthroughs — the kind depicted in cartoons by a light bulb materializing over a character's head—are more likely to happen if we have an ongoing engagement with the inner and outer worlds. Breakthroughs can signal the beginning of a project or a major advance in a work-in-progress. The light bulb may flash when we least expect it.

The idea for *Dr. Jekyl and Mr. Hyde* came to Robert Louis Stevenson in a dream. Said Stevenson, "for two days I went about racking my brains for a plot of any sort; and on the second night I dreamed the scene at the window." As an example of how alternating periods of work and relaxation can stimulate creativity, psychologist Rollo May described an important insight he had that greatly advanced a project he was working on: "Late one day, putting aside my books and papers. . . . I walked down the street toward the subway. I was tired. I tried to put the whole troubling business out of my mind. About fifty feet away from the entrance to the Eighth Street station, it suddenly struck me 'out of the blue,' as the not-unfitting expression goes. . . ."

In both of these cases, a period of conscious effort preceded the breakthrough, which was followed by more work. Stevenson still had to write his novel: "All the rest was made awake, and consciously." Rollo May wouldn't have had his insight without hard work, nor would he have known what to do with it afterwards without more work. Flashes of inspiration usually have to be paid for partly in advance and the balance in installments. There's no such thing as a free light bulb.

(To those who claim that their creative work comes for free and that they do nothing to earn it other than to act as a scribe, I say, "Either you don't give yourself enough credit, or you are truly blessed.")

Creative experiences are not available only to "gifted" people. Everyone has the facility to be creative, but many don't cultivate their creativity or apply it to art. The ideal birthday gift for a friend, an interesting dinner menu, or a decorating idea might be blown into consciousness by a minor brainstorm; these are all creative experiences. Almost everyone has accomplished *something* by alternating conscious effort with relaxation: you might try futilely to think of someone's name or the title of a song, and give up, only to have the elusive words "dawn" on you while washing dishes or waiting for a bus.

Such common experiences are evidence that unconscious processes work for everyone, even if they don't result in poetic images or ideas for novels. When the conscious mind turns its attention to writing, the unconscious will also turn in that direction, and your brainstorms will take on a more literary nature.

When students are aware of unconscious processes they can understand better the value of writing outside class and of having a notebook handy for moments of high receptivity. Writer/teacher Phillip Lopate looks for "that peculiar synchronization of ear and gut" which indicates it is an optimum time for him to write. Lopate realizes both the difficulty and importance of transmitting this kind of self-knowledge to students, teaching them "the moment to write." It is also important to know the moment to interrupt writing and let the conscious mind rest from the task at hand while the unconscious, hopefully, continues to work.

Spontaneity in starting and resuming writing is difficult to achieve in most classrooms when the workshop is not in session: it would be disruptive for students to close their math books because they heard a poem coming on or because they flashed on the resolution to a story they had been struggling with in the writing workshop earlier that morning. But elementary school teachers can set aside a few minutes for writing at times when the class is in transition, particularly after periods of relaxation such as lunch and gym, when the unconscious part of the mind has less interference from the conscious part. High-school teachers can emphasize to students how important it is for writers to know their own patterns of inspiration.

Inspiration and the Unconscious — Postscript

Most of the material I discussed in this section applies to the writing of the section itself. There was one sequence when I decided to quit out of frustration for the day and go for a walk in a snowstorm, which had become increasingly inviting as the writing bogged down. Just as I put on my coat and scarf, a way of connecting two seemingly contradictory ideas popped into my mind and I returned to my desk and jotted it down. Then I got as far as the elevator when another wave of inspiration came over me. This time I took off my coat. An hour and three pages later I went for a walk, no longer frustrated.

CREATIVE QUALITIES

The following qualities are associated with creativity. Extreme doses of some of them can interfere with success in highly structured situations, but they work for students when applied to their writing.

Imagination: Most people associate having a good imagination with a capacity for wild and strange ideas. Actually, the word "imagination" is defined in part as "the act or power of forming a mental image of something not present to the senses." And my idea of a person with a good imagination is someone whose "mental images" are clear and interesting. Part of the writer's task is to translate these images into language.

Inquisitiveness: Novels and poems are often started as a result of questions about various areas of behavior and interaction. Creative activity in the sciences, social sciences, and other fields is likewise spurred by a desire to know more than one did before.

Stubbornness: Sometimes writers should not "know when to quit."

Ability to deal with the unknown: Writers, like explorers, should be willing to keep going not only *in spite of* the fact that they don't know where they are going, but *because* they're not sure where they are going.

Arrogance: I'm not sure it is desirable, but I have found that many writers are a little arrogant about their work. Perhaps this is a shield to cover the self-doubt that walks hand-in-hand with artistic activity. In any case, a small dose of arrogance makes it easier to endure criticism and indifference.

31

4

The Writing Process

TOUGH STUFF

An essential step in creating an atmosphere conducive to writing is to discuss with the class how complicated and difficult writing can be. Inform your students—just in case they don't know—that even the best writers err, falter, cross out, and are constantly reminded how hard it is to write well. In fact, good writers tend to mark up their papers *more* than others.

Some students don't realize how difficult it can be for a good writer to put down a series of flowing, effective sentences or lines of poetry. So, when these students can't write easily and / or quickly, they assume it is because they can't do it at all, and they get discouraged. Students shouldn't feel like they are inadequate because a stream of perfect phrases doesn't flow like water at the turn of a tap.

I asked a new group to tell me what problems they had with writing. One fifth-grader replied that sometimes he gets a great idea and writes very excitedly, only to discover upon reading what he has written that he has left out words and not said things as clearly as he had intended. Another student volunteered that he tends to start a lot of sentences the same way (with such phrases as "So then..."). And a third student complained that a lot of what she writes "just doesn't sound right."

These are not writing problems as much as they are symptoms of the problem with writing: It is not a one-shot deal. I pointed out to the group the classroom's exposed concrete wall, which was tattooed with grafitti, and said that if we were to put a coat of paint on the wall, some of the concrete and grafitti would still show through. "What then?" I asked.

"It would take another coat, maybe a few coats," suggested a student. And so it goes with writing: you write until the job is done; how many "coats" it takes depends on the circumstances. If at first [draft] you don't succeed — try, try again.

Advanced writers know they can't do it all at once, so they adjust their expectations accordingly, perhaps concentrating on different aspects of writing as they go along — what researcher Elsa Bartlett calls the "divide and conquer" approach. The history of Rome wasn't written in one draft.

When students try to do a whole piece of writing all at once they increase the likelihood of failure. What might be perceived by a student as a finished piece of bad writing may actually be the beginning of something *potentially* good. I tell my students about an award-winning writer who told me that he's too embarrassed to show his first drafts to anyone because "they're so bad." But he sure knows what to do to make them damn good after the first draft.

Any discussion of the difficulty of writing should be prefaced by saying that, rather than feeling intimidated by the problems, students should feel comforted at how well they do considering the complexity of the task. An understanding of the writing process can help them do even better.

FROM START TO FINISH

After decades of emphasizing product rather than process, in the last ten years education researchers have turned their attention to identifying components of the writing process. There are no formulas, but there are patterns, and several models have been presented of the phases that occur during the course of writing. I offer students the following model, which is based on a review of recent research and my own experiences as a writer and teacher. I tell them to remember, however, that the writing process differs from author to author and that each author may vary the process from piece to piece. Also, the following phases often overlap.

Throughout the writing process, the writer is constantly selecting and rejecting words and thinking associatively. Testimony given by writers on *how* they do these things is usually based on hindsight — an attempt to unravel a process that seemed to "just happen." The more you write, though, the better you get at having good things "just happen."

PHASES OF THE WRITING PROCESS

Prewriting. Prewriting includes "getting into the mood" and mulling—sifting and sorting through potential material. This phase may occur while you are staring out the window, talking to yourself, pacing, washing dishes, or rolling a pencil back and forth. During this time an embryo is forming; you may not know what, but you sense that *something* alive will emerge.

Prewriting can involve more than this. For Mozart, the "prewriting" phase of musical composing was crucial, taking "place in a pleasing, lively dream." As he described it, sometimes he would start humming a "morsel," which would work itself into a "good dish"; the subject would eventually "enlarge itself" until the composition was almost complete in his mind. When he finally wrote the composition down, it rarely differed from what he had "heard" in his mind. Poet Larry Zirlin once commented similarly, "I wrote a poem on the subway today. Now I just have to put it on paper."

Prewriting can consist merely of coming up with an opening phrase or a tentative plan of attack — anything to break down the iciness of the cold white page. Some writers ease slowly into writing, while others skip prewriting and jump right in (similar to how different people enter a swimming pool). Many students do not realize that they may need an incubation period before they begin writing and that they should not feel pressured to get started right away. It's our job to help them understand this, and we should avoid admonishing, or helping, students who have not begun to write when in fact they may be engaged in prewriting.

Exploratory Writing. For many writers, exploratory writing is partly incorporated into the prewriting phase. Those who do little or no prewriting, however, get right down to exploring on paper. During the exploratory draft, writers find it helpful to concentrate on what they are saying, without consciously diverting energy into grammar, punctuation, sentence structure, or overall form. Also, they suppress such self-critical thoughts as, "This idea isn't worth much" or "This image doesn't seem appropriate." Poet William Carlos Williams referred to the "anarchical phase of writing" as a time when the mind is "fluid" and "every form of resistance to a complete release should be abandoned." Although it may be easy to walk and chew gum at the same time, it is extremely difficult for the mind to think creatively and critically at once.

Many writers find that "freewriting"—also called "automatic writing" or "brainstorming" — is a good technique for exploratory writing. Freewriting consists of writing non-stop without pausing or looking back, usually for a set time period. If writers get stuck, they can write, "I don't know what to write" or "I'm stuck" or they can write about their physical environment ("My toe itches" or "I hear a siren outside"). The idea is to keep the creative juices flowing, to get the synapses buzzing and the neurons humming.

Freewriting is a device to help writers get down those often-elusive first words, one of the biggest problems writers face. Students of mine have started first drafts with phrases like, "I don't know how to start this, but I'll try...." This is fine; anything that gets them going should be tried.

Students need to be reminded that they will not be held accountable for their exploratory drafts. I have often been asked, "Do you mind if I write messy on the first draft?" No, I assure them, my main concern is that they *write*. Period.

Developmental Writing. During this phase, the material is shaped. In sculpting a figure, this would be the stage when, after the large chunks had been hacked out of the stone, the face would acquire its expression and the body its stance. In writing, authors become more conscious of language and structure as they develop and connect ideas. They remain open to expansion and change, but they narrow in on the finished product. Williams referred to the piece of writing at this stage as an "object for the liveliest attention that the full mind can give. . . . " The developmental phase may span several drafts.

Developmental writing encompasses the first stage of a two-tiered revision process, which writer / teacher Donald Murray calls "internal" and "external" revision. As Murray sees it, internal revision includes "everything writers do to discover and develop what they have to say, beginning with the reading of a completed first draft."

During developmental writing, authors decide what they want to say, and they make alterations to ensure that they are saying it in the best way possible to meet the demands of the particular piece. A telegram would demand clarity and succinctness. A poem might also demand clarity and succinctness, but other concerns could include rhythm, imagery, and irony.

At the end of this stage I read the piece in search of discrepancies between what I hope I have written and what I've actually written. Then I try to make the two congruent (unless I decide I like what is actually there better than what I had intended).

External Revision. External revision occurs when the writer has accomplished either what he / she set out to accomplish or something that crystallized along the way. In the final stage of revision, writers make their work presentable to the "reading public." They pay particular attention to grammar, punctuation, and sentence structure. This is the time for fine tuning, when writers reach for their dictionaries and usage books. According to Murray, "Writers now pay attention to the conventions of form and language, mechanics, and style."

Last Look. After I have completed a piece of writing, I let it sit for a while —an hour, a day, or longer—before taking a last look. An error or an alternative way of saying something may become apparent.

An analogy for this multilayered writing process is searching for gold. First, you wander around, looking at maps and squinting into the horizon for a likely source. You might start to dig in three or four places before you actually strike gold. Perhaps some of it is fool's gold, but you gather up everything that looks like gold, even letting some sand and pebbles get into the bag, because it is getting dark and you don't want to leave anything valuable behind. You'll sort it out later. Once you've isolated the gold, it must be refined, carefully crafted into beautiful and / or useful objects (rings, coins, chains), and polished.

As I have indicated, no one model of the writing process can capture how everyone writes. One student may take ten minutes to toss and turn words before putting any down on paper, while another may write rapidly from the word "go." The former, when he/she finally gets down to writing, may have little rewriting to do, while the latter may just be beginning to toss and turn words after the first draft is done.

The model I've given is a point of reference. In actuality, the writing process may not proceed in a linear way from start to finish. Writers often move forward and backward among the various stages as they work on a text. Let's assume a writer is in the middle of the process; he/she may go back and do some more exploratory writing on a certain point. Or, exploratory writing may be interrupted by a jump forward to refine an awkward sentence. Students should be cautious about constantly jumping forward to external revision, however; not only can this break the flow of writing, but they might spend ten minutes working on one sentence, only to decide to delete the sentence later on. Sometimes I just feel like doing it, though, and then I follow my instincts.

What we write not only governs what we will write next in that writing is a constant process of discovery and unfolding as a piece develops, but it may also affect what we have written previously. We may, for example, have to go back and change something in light of an idea or image that is born farther down the writing road. A student wrote a character into a precarious situation; the only escape was through a tunnel, which the writer had to go back and "dig" in a previous paragraph.

From Start to Finish — Postscript

Here is a case study of the process by which I completed a very modest writing task.

I received a phone call from a college where I was to give a speech; they needed a title for my talk by the next day so they could put it into the program. An easy writing assignment, no more than a few words, and I had twenty-four hours to do it.

I couldn't think of anything. Twenty hours of prewriting.

Part of the problem was that I wasn't sure what I wanted to say. By the middle of the next afternoon I knew I wanted to talk in my speech about some of the things that go on when one writes, and I came up with my first draft: "The Process of Writing." But I didn't like the word "process" because it seemed to limit the scope of the talk to steps taken while writing; I also wanted to talk about the spirit of writing.

I gave up for a while and went to take a shower. While I was showering, a better word "popped" into my head (or, more precisely, "out of" my head): "The *Experience* of Writing." That was close. It said what I wanted to say, but it needed some external revision to get rid of the cumbersome preposition.

Thus, "The Writing Experience." Three modest words, just before deadline.

STUDENT WRITERS

Length and Speed. When responding to assignments, some students equate "longer" with "better," as in, "You only wrote *one* page? I'm up to five and still going." Hopefully, those five pages will be wonderful, but chances are there's a lot of filler. Even if the five pages were airtight, this story wouldn't necessarily be superior to a one-page story.

An assignment handled admirably in eight lines by one student may evoke an epic poem or long story in another student. Knowing how far to take a piece of work is a quality that cannot be taught but which should be discussed.

Unless they are writing under deadline, speed should not be a factor; students should not feel pressured to beat each other to the final punctuation mark. Many students feel a sense of accomplishment in being first to finish *anything* in class, as if each activity were a race in which the first hand shooting up signalled victory. I once heard an early finisher moan condescendingly, "Are you still working?" to a classmate who was agonizing over whether or not to eliminate the first line of her poem and whether to add a simile to the fourth line. "Yes, and proud of it," was her reply.

Sometimes five minutes after I give a complicated assignment, a student will throw down his/her pencil with authoritative finality and announce, "I'm done." My reply is usually, "Let's see about that." It is possible that a delightful, complete piece has been written, but more likely there has been an attempt to traverse conception to completion in two or three perfunctory steps.

Spontaneity. The rules of the game are different for creative writing than they are for many other classroom tasks — the writing workshop needs openness and flexibility by students and teacher alike. Most history questions and math problems are laid out so that the students know exactly what is expected of them, and there is usually a correct response. It doesn't work that way with good creative writing assignments, which invite trying individual approaches. Students have usually been taught to be concerned with following instructions, a necessary behavior in many endeavors. Being overly concerned with the instructions for a writing assignment, however, can interfere with the creative process.

Because of the large number of students in most classes, the pressures of the school day, and the convenience of having everyone work on the same thing at the same time and finish together so they can proceed to the next order of business, it is tempting to use a stimulus/response approach to teaching writing. This would consist of presenting a highly structured writing assignment, followed by execution of that assignment. Unfortunately, this kind of approach can also "execute" creative impulses. On the other hand, if you encourage your students not to give equal time to each assignment and to consider changes in direction, you help them learn to make artistic commitments based on internal needs instead of external demands.

Pity the creative writer whose mind doesn't wander! One fascinating aspect of artistic venture is that the work can change shape and direction right before your eyes. Students should be open to the possibility of turning off of the main boulevard of an assignment in order to explore the side streets. Changing horses in midstream might mean getting wet, but it also might result in finding an interesting place you hadn't considered visiting when you set out on your journey. Poet/teacher Richard Hugo makes the distinction between what triggers a piece of writing and what is generated during the course of writing: "A poem can be said to have two subjects, the initiating or triggering subject, which starts the poem or 'causes' the poem to be written, and the real or generated subject, which the poem comes to say or mean, and which is generated or discovered in the poem during the writing." The stimulus that gets a poem or story started might become less important as the piece progresses and might not even appear in the final version.

Some pieces of writing suffer because the author knew too much, too soon. Such writing can convey a feeling that the issues had been settled and the tension resolved before the pen even reached the paper. There was no confrontation, just a distanced recording. I am not saying that all writing experiences should be full of changes in direction and surprises, but that students are often better off being faithful to their own creative impulses than to an assignment or even to the first few lines of a piece. Before I started encouraging students to pursue opportunities suggested in the course of their writing and not worry so much about doing the assignment "correctly," there would often be one student who, after hearing others read their work out loud, would be reluctant to share his/her poem because, "I goofed up and did it wrong." Usually this student had actually done an interesting piece of writing, perhaps even suggesting a new twist on the assignment or a new topic entirely.

Here is an excerpt from a student who started responding to an assignment to link exaggerated physical actions with emotions and ended up on another planet:

> I'm so mad at my brother that I could punch him out into space. Now my idiotic brother is zooming in space getting nowhere but finally he lands on a weird planet named Lunatic....
> —Rachel Satyabhashak

Rachel didn't go too much further with this story. But, if days after the other students had finished their poems about their emotions, Rachel had been deep into a science fiction story, I wouldn't have admonished her for not following directions. On the contrary, I would have been glad that my assignment had enabled her to generate something truly her own.

Robin Snow, a sixth-grader whose name is a poem itself, described an experience with change of direction: "One time I started to write a composition and for some reason right then and there it turned into a poem. It seemed like the composition went the way *it* wanted, not the way I wanted. It was like some powerful force had taken over." This "powerful force" comes so rarely to writers that it would be a shame to resist, without at least giving the force a chance to "put up or shut up." Not every powerful force turns into a great piece of writing, but the least one can do is hear it out.

Distractions occur all the time: Sometimes while talking to a friend, watching a movie, or sitting in a writing workshop, we find ourselves "somewhere else." A phrase keeps turning around silently on our tongue; we picture someone we haven't thought about in years; a fantasy unfolds; or there is something so urgent going on in our life that it's difficult for anything else to command our attention. Distractions should be treated similarly to changes in direction. They are differentiated from changes in direction in that they don't emanate directly from the text. Students should be encouraged to track down these distractions and write about them, even if it means dropping an assignment in mid-sentence or not even starting it at all.

Now that I have extolled the virtues of spontaneity, let me pull back a little. While detours and distractions can be beneficial to follow, students should not become *too* fickle. Constant straying from the task at hand may be a symptom of an inability to sustain a writing idea.

Discipline. One of the traits necessary for success in any field—especially the arts—is the resolve to stick with something. Sometimes the path is lined with difficulties and exhaustion, common roadblocks in the writing process.

Students sometimes drop their work in mid-writing—or never get started —because of frustration aroused by trying to cope with disconcerting or unwieldy material or because of mental exhaustion. Although it can be helpful to put away a difficult piece for a time or to rest for a while and re-

39

charge their batteries, students should not become predisposed to avoidance or a pattern of laziness. It is important for them to learn when to "hang in there" and persist until they either succeed or are convinced that a poem or story cannot be realized, at least not now. This sense of whether to pause, persist, or desist comes from a self-awareness gleaned from experience.

My own method with a difficult piece is to work on it in spurts—sporadic "sneak attacks." But at some point I usually make a sustained effort during which I try not to let my mind or body wander away from the boundaries of the paper in front of me. When the going gets tough, though, many students get going—to the garbage can. This is one reason why I ask them not to throw away anything they write. It is possible to botch something so badly that they are better off with a fresh start, but students are more likely to be running away from the disorder that has appeared on the paper. Sometimes, when the disorder is *only* in appearance—cross-outs and sloppy handwriting—students need to be reminded that neatness is not a virtue on a rough draft. Other times, the disorder goes deeper than appearance: the content is messy. Being creative involves trying to find an order in disorder, to shape it into something meaningful and/or beautiful. Psychologist Rollo May points out that "mathematicians and physicists talk about the 'elegance' of a theory." Often this elegance emerges out of a jumble of numbers, signs, and ideas.

As for dealing with exhaustion, this is a matter of getting to know one's writing self. Certainly, we need rest, but there are times when my best writing comes when I think I have nothing left but decide to plow ahead and see what happens.

Many people have the image of creative writers and other artists as freewheeling and spontaneous, working when they get the whim until the whim runs out. This, thankfully, is the way it is *sometimes.* But most serious artists are capable of great discipline and often devote long stretches of concentrated effort to their work. When working with students, we must be careful not to give them the impression that artistic expression is always natural and fun; otherwise, when they find out for themselves how much hard work is involved they will conclude either that *we* don't know much about what it's really like or that *they* must not be very good at it.

My students write mostly short pieces. I encourage them to try at least one long poem, extended short story, and/or play, for the experience of having an ongoing involvement with a writing project. Through this involvement, they will become familiar with and learn to cope with the inevitable roadblocks.

There is another reason for discussing the importance of discipline in writing, and I would be remiss not to deal with it both in my workshops and in this book. A writing workshop should encourage individualized written expression, but this approach conflicts with many writing tasks that confront students. Take the essay question on an exam (as Henny Youngman would add, "Please!"): The student has a time limit, perhaps as little as ten minutes, so there is insufficient time for prewriting; if the student stares out the window searching for inspiration for ten minutes, it's all over. The time limit also eliminates the opportunity for much revision; there is hardly enough time for one draft. If the student does revise directly on the exam (crossing out and inserting), the paper will appear to be "messy," which may have a negative effect on the teacher, for whom grading exam questions is tedious enough without having to decipher a tangle of cross-outs and arrows. Finally, if in the middle of an essay question on the causes of World War I, the student has a great insight about the League of Nations and pursues this change of direction, he/she will lose points for "not answering the question."

Is this, then, an admission that if you follow the advice in this book your students will be ill-prepared to deal with other writing activities, that they will become spoiled and temperamental "artistes"? No way. (Aren't you relieved? I know I am.) The more someone's confidence is built up and the more mastery they feel over language the more capable they become of handling *any* writing task. Much of what students do in the workshop can feed into other tasks: What teacher wouldn't welcome a composition that had some life and a sense of voice? What college admissions officer wouldn't be impressed by an application autobiography that used clear language and imagery and read like a short story?

Professional writers, especially journalists, often have to write under pressure and conform to someone else's standards. We should help students to understand that there are certain times when they have to play by someone else's rules and that they should work toward becoming confident, skillful writers who can deliver under any circumstances. This confidence is fostered by having successful experiences with open-ended writing and also by doing occasional "discipline drills" — assignments that must be completed, strictly following directions, within a given time period. A confident basketball player might say, "I'll go one-on-one with anybody. Anywhere." A confident writer would say, "I'll write anything for anybody. Anytime."

Students should come to feel like writers, not writing machines that need to be programmed before they can function. This means they must learn how to deal with making decisions about their writing, including when and how to be spontaneous and disciplined and to adapt to external factors.

GOOD STUFF

We should not let students underestimate the difficulty of writing well, but neither should we dwell excessively on the difficulty. Writing is like a pet that sometimes sits around and mopes and sometimes growls and snaps, but which can be a great companion, and, with care and patience, do some amazing tricks.

There are moments of pure writing, when you feel as if you are both the writer and the reader at the same time: when you find the phrase that expresses exactly what you have been trying to say or says something unexpected but appropriate that leads you to think "Wow!...but of course!"; when a character in a story says something so remarkable that you giggle with your own success; when a startling image jumps out of you and onto the page. Sometimes perfection comes in simplicity. Kafka wrote in his diary, "When I arbitrarily write a single sentence, for instance, 'He looked out of the window,' it already has perfection."

Writing can function as merely a means to an end, but it can also be an end in itself. Sometimes it's palatable at best, other times it's downright delicious. Writing is an imprecise craft, erratic and sporadic; you pray for intervention in the form of inspiration, but you must contribute discipline and sweat. You may be in the midst of writing and feel exhausted. You don't think it will ever come together. Then, a breakthrough, and it is finished. And it remains forever. I don't always like writing, but I usually love having written.

Poet Frank O'Hara once said, "...at times when I would rather be dead the thought that I could never write another poem has so far stopped me."

5

Form and Content

COMMON ELEMENTS

Titles. Sometimes a student will ask before writing anything, "Do I need a title?" Or a student who is having trouble getting started will say it's because, "I can't think of a title." Although authors sometimes start with a title (which might be changed in light of the finished work), thinking of a title should never be considered an issue until a piece is done. Even then, for poetry the answer to "Do I need a title?" is "Not unless you want one." E. E. Cummings, for example, numbered his poems, and many other poets have used the first line of a poem as the title or simply called a poem "Poem."

These are accepted conventions for poetry, but stories almost always have titles. If a student is stuck, advise him/her to use any title for the time being, as an appropriate one will probably emerge later.

Titles can serve different functions:

1. provide information necessary to the poem or story, such as setting the scene ("On My Way To Work," "Midsummer");
2. "label" the piece, in which case the title should be unobtrusive ("The Argument");
3. be a phrase that works as an adjunct to the text, perhaps an image you weren't able to "work in";
4. emphasize a particular image, when it is a word or phrase taken directly from the text.

Such abstract titles as "Reflections" and "Existence" are best avoided, as well as titles that explain what the poem or story is about to say. I once changed a title from "The Arbitrariness of It All" to "Hands," because an editor pointed out that my original title stated the "meaning" of the poem. "Hands," on the other hand, referred to the poem's central image.

The Literary Body. Poet/teacher Joel Oppenheimer gave our graduate school workshop a lecture on structure, which I memorized and have repeated verbatim to many classes. I quote it here in its entirety:

> Every poem (or story) has a beginning, a muddle, and an end.

That's all that one can say for sure, but I will expand on this lecture with some general comments about these three parts of the literary body.

The beginning of any piece of writing is crucial. It should *involve* the reader in some way. This could be, metaphorically speaking, by grabbing the reader by the shoulders and shouting, "Listen here, this is urgent," or by gently taking the reader's hand and whispering, "Come here." The opening could be an arresting image, an intriguing piece of dialogue, or a description of scenery that will lift the reader out of his/her chair and into the written landscape. The beginning can be anything, but it should be good. As the Godfather might say, "Your opening should be an offer the reader can't refuse."

———

Endings should leave the reader feeling like he/she has *experienced* something. If there are loose ends, the reader should feel that the author is aware of them and that they are not the results of carelessness. The degree of closure, or resolution, can vary. Some pieces have a firm sense of closure: an extreme case would be a story in which every conflict is resolved and the characters "live happily ever after" (or, at the other extreme, where all the characters are run over by a bus). Poems and stories with weak closure seem to have been scissored at mid-piece; the reader may turn the page looking for more. E. E. Cummings was demonstrative about using weak closure in some of his poems, ending them with unclosed parentheses or ellipses.

Many contemporary writers lean away from strong closure. The objective of a particular poem or story may be to articulate certain questions without answering them, or to convey a state of mind or a situation. It's acceptable to leave the reader hanging, as long as the writer provides something to hang onto. Not every conflict needs to be resolved, but something should be revealed.

Some students think that strong closure is required, an attitude that may come from having read so many stories with endings like, "And everyone lived happily ever after" or "And so with all the town's problems solved, the stranger rode off into the sunset." We should introduce student writers to a flexible approach to closure. Without the burden of having to make every piece of writing resolve into a definitive, final statement, writing becomes a less intimidating prospect.

———

Not much in general can be said about the "muddle," except that it must emanate from the beginning and work itself into the ending. Each piece of writing assumes its own identity, which indicates the best way to proceed.

POETRY

Poems and Prose Poems. I have never been able to come up with a satisfactory definition of poetry. In that I am not alone. A. E. Housman wrote that when he was asked to define "poetry," he "replied that I could no more define poetry than a terrier can define a rat, but that I thought we both recognized the object by the symptoms which it provokes in us." References to the elements of poetry — highly charged language, rhythm, and metaphor—could apply as well to literary prose as to poetry. As W. H. Auden said, ". . . it is a sheer waste of time to look for a definition of the difference between poetry and prose." In this age of free verse, people usually accept the notion that poetry is differentiated from prose mostly by the way it appears on the page. Linebreaks make a piece of writing *look* like a poem, even if—due to a lack of rhyme and meter—it doesn't *sound* like the poems in our older textbooks.

Okay, so if it has linebreaks, then it's a poem. But, you might ask, "What do you call the many pieces that students write consisting of a paragraph (or two or three)? These can't be short stories because they lack the ingredients associated with fiction (character development, plot, etc.), and they aren't essays. Surely, they're not *poems*; getting rid of rhyme and meter is one thing, but wouldn't it be going too far to throw out linebreaks, too?"

Well, these pieces of writing *are* poems. Sort of. They can be called "prose poems." This is not "newspeak." The prose poem is a legitimate and popular literary form. Poet Michael Benedikt has edited a large anthology called *The Prose Poem*, which contains selections from many countries. In his introduction, Benedikt points out that the prose poem has been an important genre worldwide for almost two centuries, although English-speaking poets have only begun recently to use the form extensively.

Over the last dozen years or so, many American poetry magazines, anthologies, and collections by individual poets have included prose poems. Many students write prose poems naturally, while having to cultivate a taste for linebreaks. These young prose poets are, unbeknownst to themselves, part of a literary trend.

45

I am no more inclined to tender a definition of the prose poem than I am of poetry. Any definition is liable to sound fuzzy or not to hold up in all cases. Prose poems are usually brief; but John Ashbery's book *Three Poems* is prose, divided into three sections, ranging from 11 to 53 pages in length. Russell Edson, one of the most widely published American prose poets, calls the prose poem "a funny fish-fowl," adding that "the special freedom that the prose poem has, and its special charm, is its quickness." Edson's prose poems are highly inventive and accomplish their business rapidly, while others' prose poems are more realistic and/or discursive.

Benedikt states that the only feature that absolutely distinguishes prose poems from verse poems (poems with linebreaks) is they don't have line-breaks. Why, then, are they called poems? I have often responded to this question with the following quotation attributed to blues singer Big Bill Broonzy, who, when asked how the songs *he* wrote could be called "folk songs," replied, "Never heard a horse sing 'em." (I have heard a similar story featuring Louis Armstrong.) This anecdote usually gets a laugh from teachers, who understand my point: "Who cares what you *call* them— poems, prose poems, or Alfreds? A rose by any other name, etc." The borderline between prose and poetry is often indistinct or nonexistent. Many poets write poems that, without linebreaks, would be straight prose, and many fiction writers use a disjointed approach to language that is usually associated with some styles of poetry. Many writers, myself included, move easily among forms—verse poems, prose poems, and fiction —depending on which form is appropriate for a given piece.

If professional writers are becoming less and less concerned with classifications, why make a fuss about them with students? I usually request that my workshops be billed as "creative writing" rather than "poetry" workshops, in order to avoid getting bogged down in the discussion of labels. My major concern in teaching is the marriage of language to emo-tional, experiential, and imaginative impulses. There can be no illegitimate offspring.

Sometimes, as I am giving an assignment, I say, "All right, now it's time to write your poems." And a student will ask, "Does it have to be a *poem*?" I explain that I often use the word "poem" to indicate any piece of creative writing, just as some jazz musicians refer to any instrument as a "horn." I once showed my guitar to a jazz musician, who responded, "Nice horn." I knew what he meant. I never heard a horse play one.

Rhyme. The vast majority of contemporary poets do not work with rhyme schemes, but the fact that rhyming is out of fashion (actually, it's making a small comeback) is not why I don't encourage students to use it. It takes a lot of skill and experience to use rhyme effectively. While it is possible to write excellent rhyming poetry (Yeats, for one, did pretty well), it is far more common for young students to write bad rhyming poetry, lapsing into singsong rhythms and nonsensical statements for which the only justifica-tion is the rhyme.

Without rhyming, on the other hand, students tend to turn out work that is more interesting, imaginative, and truly felt. In the few instances when students believe they can write better poetry using rhyme, I request that they try not rhyming also and see which approach they like better. I might ask a student to rewrite a rhyming poem without using rhymes, to get him/her to explore more possibilities.

I've found the following analogy useful in explaining the limitation that rhyming puts on word usage: "It is like moving into an apartment building and looking for a new friend, but limiting your search to those who live on the third floor. Appropriate words, like good friends, are hard to find, and it would be a shame to pass one by because it doesn't rhyme." Consider the following:

She was sitting under the tree looking cute
As I walked by she offered me a piece of fruit

The author is unable to be specific, since "pear" and "grape" do not rhyme with "cute" (and she could never offer an "orange" since that doesn't rhyme with anything).

Also, a writer unskilled in prosody will often wind up with awkward inversions in order to place the rhyming word at the end of the line:

I shot the ball and it went in
And the game our team did win!

Instead, this writer could have used a more natural sounding construction:

I shot the ball and it went in.
Our team won the game!

Without the need to conform to a rhyme scheme, a simile could have been added:

I shot the ball and it went in
like a trained dog through a hoop.
Our team won the game!

The notion that rhyming can get in the way of saying what you want to say is dealt with playfully by Marjorie Fleming, who wrote about the death of James II (quoted by Babette Deutsch in *Poetry Handbook*):

He was killed by a cannon splinter,
Quite in the middle of the winter;
Perhaps it was not at that time,
But I can get no other rhyme.

I would add that if James II had been killed by the entire cannonball, Fleming no doubt would have made it happen "quite in the middle of the fall."

47

Rhyme—Postscript

THE RHYME/SONG

Rhyming has its charm and appeal
So when I am writing and I feel
Like making up a rhyme or two
I don't let it get me blue

I just take the notion
And whip up a musical potion
Putting rhymes where they belong
In the lyrics of a song

CHORUS: The sound's been around
     Since the days of the lyre
     And there's really no need
     For it to retire

     Rhymes please the ear and the memory
     But I'd rather that you sing
     Than recite them to me

Language. Although many poems contain words that seem to have been plucked from lofty perches, most contemporary poets utilize the cadences and diction of common speech. This doesn't mean, however, that everything spoken could be a poem. While it is true that anyone is capable of uttering something that, if written down, would be poetic, these kernels of speech are usually surrounded by mundane, nonevocative language. Writers who use the vernacular apply a great deal of skill to achieve a natural, yet dramatic, style. It takes uncommon care to write in a common way.

After one of my poetry readings, someone came up to me and expressed surprise that poetry could sound so "normal." "That's nice," he said, "you just write that stuff down the way you would say it." Oh, if he only knew how much revision is necessary to get writing to sound spontaneous. Interviews that are published verbatim tend to be wordy and awkward; skillful editing is required for an interview to retain its conversational tone and to make smooth reading without distorting anything in the process.

The writer must elevate the common idiom by exploiting its liveliness, expressiveness, musicality, and directness, while eschewing its tedium. In short, writers make common speech as good as it can be.

Here is a poem by Gay Phillipps in the voice of a woman who works in a dry-goods store. Perhaps this poem is an exact transcription of something the woman actually said, but more likely it is a skillful distillation of what she said or a fabricated version of what the woman *might* have said. Whichever it is, the poem makes for good reading:

THE LADY WHO WORKS
the lady who works
in the G&B Dry
Goods said to me I've got
to get rid of my flowers
they take up too much time
there's a lot you have
to do for um y'know
and I have almost an acre
of lawn now too   my
niece she just kept mowin' it
back and mowin' it back   I
mowed it myself the other
day   I'm alone y'know
can't find anyone
to do it anymore so I
did it myself and
afterward I sat down
on the back step and
I'm tellin' you I felt
like some rich bitch
I said to myself you
don't have anything
but you sure do
have a yard

Many people have written off poetry because they were turned off by the formal diction used in the poetry they encountered in old school textbooks, a language that seemed distant and aloof. When I bring contemporary poetry into high-school and adult writing classes, students often respond that "these don't sound like poems," amazed that poetry can speak directly to them, rather than float above their heads. I am pleased that recent literary developments have made poetry more accessible, but I am not happy that it has become somewhat fashionable to disparage indiscriminately "stuffy, old-fashioned poetry" while extolling the virtues of modern, colloquial poetry. Some writing teachers do this in an effort to change the negative attitudes many students have toward poetry, hoping to make students more receptive to the notion of writing as well as reading it.

This is understandable on a tactical level, especially at the beginning of a high-school workshop, when long-lived prejudices against poetry may have to be broken down quickly. But students should be made aware that the best traditional poems are rich and awesome in their emotion, imagination, ideas, *and* language. Students don't have to emulate these poems in their own writing, but they can appreciate them, especially when these traditional poems are not taught as literary cadavers to be dissected but rather as living specimens created by men and women in an attempt to say something.

I have come across some high-school students who attempt to sound "Poetic" with a capital "P" by using language they would never use in conversation. Sometimes, these students have been complimented on their writing because their poetry *sounds* the way some people think poems are supposed to, even though the poems may not be particularly well done. These students are usually disappointed when I suggest that they exchange some of their highfalutin words and phrases for simpler language. It's not that I have anything against fancy words, but students often do not have the command of language to use them, and the result can be as awkward as an ill-fitting, unmatched tuxedo. If you want to walk gracefully on stilts, you have to know what you're doing. This doesn't mean that students shouldn't take chances with words and try to increase their command of the language, but an unusual word should only be used instead of a common one when there is something about its sound or meaning that makes it more appropriate for the particular situation. It is not a crime for a writer to show off, but he/she should have something worth showing.

Language—Postscript

An actress friend of mine was feeling insecure about an upcoming production because she was afraid she would look pale in comparison to others in the cast who seemed flashier on stage. A critic praised her performance, saying that "every economical gesture and expression radiates simplicity and conviction...." A piece of writing that does likewise can be more effective than a bombastic, showy piece. I lean toward the power of "simplicity and conviction," both as a reader and a writer, and only use pomp when the circumstance warrants.

Movement. Most poems are composed by association. One thing leads to another, and another, and so on. This associating can reflect the poet's contemplation of thoughts and feelings (sometimes directed to a "you" who doesn't get a word in edgewise) or it can represent a description or narrative. Charles Reznikoff compressed a classic example of associative thinking into two lines:

The nail is lost. Perhaps the shoe;
horse and rider; kingdom, too.

Movement through a poem can range from small steps to what poet Robert Bly calls "leaps." Bly has written about the importance of leaping in poetry, which he defines as "the ability to associate fast....the considerable distance between the associations, the distance the spark has to leap, gives the lines their bottomless feeling, their space, and the speed of the association increases the excitement of the poetry."

"The Open Window," a poem by Tomas Transtromer (translated from the Swedish by Robert Bly), demonstrates the excitement of associative leaping:

THE OPEN WINDOW

I shaved one morning standing
by the open window
on the second story.
Switched on the razor.
It started to hum.
A heavier and heavier whirr.
Grew to a roar.
Grew to a helicopter.
And a voice—the pilot's—pierced
the noise, shouting:
"Keep your eyes open!
You're seeing this for the last time!"
Rose.
Floated low over the summer.
The small things I love, what do they amount to?
So many variations of green.
And especially the red of housewalls.
Beetles glittered in the dung, in the sun.
Cellars pulled up by the roots
sailed through the air.
Industry.
Printing presses crawled along.
People at that instant
were the only things motionless.
They held their minute of silence.
And the dead in the churchyard especially
held still
like those who posed in the infancy of the camera.
Fly low!
I didn't know which way
to turn my head—
my sight was divided
like a horse's.

By associating the sound of the electric razor with that of a helicopter, Transtromer introduces an integral image into the poem.

You can explain the concept of leaping to students by equating it with their dreams, which often leap about. In writing, a sense of leaping—or, as Bly puts it when the jump isn't as far, "hopping"—can be arrived at by following the natural associations of the mind, utilizing unconscious thought processes. It can also be attained in revision by eliminating transitional phrases.

Comedy is another area that utilizes various degrees of association. Ask students to listen carefully to comedians on television. Some monologues display linear association—each subject smoothly segues into the next— while others move by leaps and bounds. Individual jokes can benefit from skipping about, as indicated by comedian Rodney Dangerfield:

Ya gotta go from one to three, y'know? Like, a joke is like one, two, three, but if you give 'em two, that's the time to think, it loses the zing, know what I mean? Ya go one–three, they have to put it together themselves, ya leave out two, right? They figure it out, they go 'Aha!' *They're* smart! Then they like ya even more. With a really sophisticated audience you can go from one to four and leave out two *and* three.

The Line. When one is writing with a set meter, linebreaks are predetermined. When you reach your quota of feet you move on to the next line. But in free verse there are no "inherited" lines; each poem has its own rhythm and shape, and each linebreak is a decision.

The linebreak is literally a break in the line: the flow of words gets split, usually before it reaches the right-hand margin, and it continues on the next line until it gets broken again. And so on. A line of poetry can be as short as one word, or it can extend beyond the right-hand margin, in which case the overrun is indented to indicate that it is not a new line:

This is an example of a word flow that just keeps
coming at you in one poetic line and makes
you read quickly it doesn't want to be broken
and lose its frenetic flow till suddenly it can't
hold on any longer and it
bursts, spilling onto the next line
and the next
slowing
you
down.

A line can stop at a grammatical pause,
and then go on to the next line.
This is an *endstop*.
Or, a line can
be broken right in the
middle of a grammatical
unit — this is called
enjambment.
A grammatical pause may occur
during a line. This is called a *caesura*.

The linebreak is one of the poet's most important resources, yet most poets talk in the vaguest terms about how they break lines, often saying in effect, "I do it the way I feel like doing it." Early in a workshop I tell students to do likewise and use their instincts when breaking lines; I want them to concentrate on *what* they are writing. Later on, when they are more experienced, we discuss linebreaks.

When linebreaks are used well, they enhance a poem's overall effect, shaping the poem and giving it a sensuous appearance on the page. Generally, linebreaks cause readers to proceed more slowly and, perhaps, attentively than they might when reading prose. This William Carlos Williams poem would lose a lot without its shape:

THE RED WHEELBARROW

So much depends
upon

a red wheel
barrow

glazed with rain
water

beside the white
chickens

When a word or phrase is isolated on a line, it forms a unit that is both self-contained and interconnected with neighboring lines, an effect that cannot be achieved in prose: "So much depends upon a red wheelbarrow glazed with rainwater beside the white chickens."

There are no guidelines for how to break lines, no accepted rules, but there are some ways of approaching the task and some exercises to help students get a feel for "the line."

You can think of the linebreak as an additional form of punctuation available to poets. Poet Denise Levertov has called the linebreak "half a comma." But the linebreak is unlike the comma and other punctuation marks in that its use is not dictated by grammar. Whereas a comma, semicolon, or period usually indicate a grammatical separation, the poet can cluster words via a linebreak for reasons other than a grammatical imperative. Linebreaks can create rhythmic pauses, although these pauses may be subliminal at times.

Some poets think of linebreaks as being determined by the poet's "breath." Poet Charles Olson said, "And the line comes (I swear it) from the breath, from the breathing of the man who writes, at the moment that he writes...." This notion is difficult to explain in practical terms—basically, it's the "I do it the way I feel like doing it" attitude. But it is useful in that it emphasizes a noncerebral, "gut" approach: the writer pays attention to the natural rhythms that are generated by the act of composition.

Sometimes a poem is essentially prose broken into lines, with conventional sentence structure and punctuation. Other times, the use of linebreaks as punctuation enables the poet to dispense with connective words and some, or all, punctuation. Here's a prose paragraph:

As I look outside, I can see the trees sway. They look like dancers. There are also flowers that climb quietly as the kind rain falls.

This paragraph could be put into verse, minus connective words and punctuation:

outside
trees sway like dancers
flowers quietly climb

kind
rain
falls

The backdrop of the blank page can be part of the poem. In addition to being able to end anywhere, a line can *start* anywhere; although most poets tend to begin each line at the left-hand margin and only skip lines for stanza breaks, poets can also use such spatial devices as indentation, skipping spaces, and skipping lines:

    outside

trees sway   dancers
    flowers quietly   climb

   kind

       rain

         falls

A word or phrase can be spotlighted by being given its own line, and the spotlight can be made brighter by leaving the line above and/or below blank.

When I write, I shape the poem instinctively as I compose, then refine the linebreaks during revision, perhaps with a more conscious effort toward achieving specific effects. Sometimes, I start writing with linebreaks and realize that the piece is being inhibited by the form, so I switch to prose; other times, the opposite occurs.

Basically, I do it the way I feel like doing it.

———■———

Here are some brief activities involving linebreaks:

Write the following sentence on the board, and ask the students to copy it, putting in their own linebreaks:

Love is not all it's cracked up to be.

One possibility is:

Love is not all
it's cracked up
to be

By putting "it's cracked up" on its own line, you get a play on words that doesn't occur when the sentence is written as prose. Another possibility is:

Love is not
all
it's cracked up to be

This arrangement shines the spotlight on the word "all."

As an alternative to the traditional notion of rhythm determined by "feet"—which are made up of syllabic units—William Carlos Williams used the metaphor of musical "beats" in discussing linebreaks. Not all musical notes—and not all syllables—are equal. (In 4/4 time, it takes eight 1/8 notes to make up four beats, but only one whole note.) Williams determined the linebreaks in some of his poems by the number of "beats." The following exercise gives students a feel for this concept.

Write the following sentence on the board:

Hey, you there on the corner, please stop, I need help.

Ask the students to break this sentence into lines, thinking of each line as having an equal number of beats, as in the following examples.

Hey
you there on the corner
please stop
I need help

*

Hey you there on the corner please stop I need
help

*

Hey
you there on the corner please stop
I
need
help

Ask students to write a one-paragraph description. Then tell them to put it into linebreaks without making any other changes.

SICK

When I feel sick it feels like the sun is in front of me. And there's no way to escape. Then it feels like the sun is cooling down and there is no sun to make me feel hot anymore. Then I feel cold, but too cold, and I want to be hot again. I don't want to be too cold or too hot. I want to be warm.

SICK
When I feel sick
it feels like the sun
is in front of me
and there's no
way to escape.
Then it feels
like the sun is cooling down
and there is no sun
to make me feel hot anymore.
Then I feel cold
but too cold
and I want to be hot again.

I don't want to be too cold
or too hot.
I want to be warm.

—Angela Fotis

Now, ask students to rewrite the same piece, dropping as many words and punctuation marks as possible, using indentation and skipping lines when helpful.

SICK

sun in front
no escape

sun cooling down
no sun
to make me hot

cold

               too cold

I want to be hot again

not too cold
  or too hot

warm

I advise students not to get caught up in too much fancy footwork on the page, trying to position every word and phrase in a "meaningful" way. Just because a device is available to the writer doesn't mean it must be used constantly. In discussing architecture, Frank Lloyd Wright said, "Form follows function," and this sentiment was echoed by poet Robert Creeley as "Form is never more than an extension of content." Students can experiment with various arrangements of words on the page, but you should point out when you feel they are emphasizing form detached from content.

The Stanza. The stanza is verse's equivalent of the paragraph. Stanza breaks, like linebreaks, are determined mostly by instinct unless the writer is working in a set form. Some practitioners of free verse occasionally utilize stanzaic structures, such as poems written in three-line stanzas. Such symmetry can have an aesthetic appeal and can remove some of the uncertainty from composing in free verse.

The Line—Postscript

When I first looked at the following poem, I thought the author—high school student Barbara Green—was playing "tricks" with the linebreaks, arbitrarily breaking lines in odd places for an "arty" effect. But when I finished the poem I realized there was a good reason for the breaks:

THE KEY

A thin stream (winter's
snow) runs down the
gutter. Naked trees
tower over the st-
reet casting shad-
ows. New songbirds
clean their nests.
As I walk the side-
walk, I am enchanted
locked out of my ho-
use writing this do-
wn on the back of
an old paycheck
stub.

This poem captures a moment when the perception for a poem erupts in stunning clarity. You can be waking up from a dream, sitting on a train, or walking down the street when a writing idea crystallizes. You don't want to lose it, so you reach for a pen and paper. If you don't have a notebook, you'll settle for anything—a napkin, the margins of a newspaper, or the back of an old paycheck stub. In this poem, form is an extension not only of content but also the physical experience of writing the poem.

It's understandable why the first draft was written with these linebreaks. "But," one might ask, "why were they kept when the poem was copied over?" The reason is that the linebreaks help capture the immediacy of the moment; the reader can visualize the author writing excitedly on the back of the paystub, darting from end to end.

Punctuation. Punctuation works in conjunction with linebreaks to comprise a series of roadsigns that guide the reader through a poem. As I have pointed out, linebreaks, blank spaces between phrases, and compressed syntax can make a lot of punctuation expendable. Some poems are punctuated in the same way as prose, while others have little or no punctuation. Poets have a great deal of leeway, but should be consistent within each poem; once they start with a certain approach to punctuation, be it maximal or minimal, they should carry it through to the end.

I ask students to be considerate. They shouldn't leave an unjustified comma lying around for the reader to trip on and shouldn't make the reader grope blindly through a dense poem made ambiguous from lack of punctuation markings to lead the way.

There are times in writing poetry when punctuation seems integral to the form. Other times punctuation intrudes, and the poem can be read fluidly without it; these poems tend to have shorter lines, more sentence fragments, and more stanza breaks than poems with a lot of punctuation.

I was once asked by a writer if I "loved" commas, periods, semicolons, and the rest. I thought it was a peculiar question at the time, but realized later that a well-placed comma or dash can be very pleasing (though I don't know if I'd call it love). The turning point in my attitude toward commas came the first time I taught restrictive and nonrestrictive clauses, using an example from Strunk and White's *Elements of Style.* Take the sentence, "People who live in glass houses shouldn't throw stones." Then add two commas, giving the sentence a nonrestrictive clause: "People, who live in glass houses, shouldn't throw stones." The meaning is transformed by those two little squiggles.

To demonstrate the punctuation possibilities of a simple line, take "She hugged him, and the trembling subsided." Alternatives are:

She hugged him; the trembling subsided.
She hugged him. The trembling subsided.
She hugged him and the trembling subsided.
She hugged him the trembling subsided.

Capitalization. Writers have more leeway in the use of capital letters in poetry than in prose. Some poets capitalize the beginning of each line, even if it is the middle of a sentence; some capitalize poetry the same way as they would prose; others have a "minimalist" approach to capital letters, using them only for proper names and the word "I," or not at all. Many poets vary their approach from poem to poem.

these lines look all right
without capital letters

There are some poets, however, who
Prefer their poetry to look this way.

I don't like the way
the first person singular pronoun
and proper names look in lower case
i know that e.e. cummings disagreed

Students should have the same flexibility
with capitalization and punctuation
that professional poets have.
The "look" of a poem is an Important Element.

Experiment with different approaches
but try to be Consistent
Within each poem.
i wouldn't use this one
As a model.

NOTES ON OTHER FORMS

Stories and Plays. Although this book does not contain a detailed discussion of short story writing, applicable material appears throughout. The basic ingredients of fiction are characterization, plot, and setting. Short stories contain dramatic tension, often in the form of a conflict, which can be between two people (Steve and John, best friends, like the same girl), within one person (Susan has to decide whether to continue pursuing a career as a concert pianist or have a more "normal" childhood), with circumstances (Betty gets lost while hiking in the woods and has to spend the night on her own), or shared conflict (a brother and sister plot to reconcile their estranged parents). The characters usually go through something that has an effect on them. Some stories have highly structured plots, while others are more episodic, presenting glimpses into the characters' lives, or place the emphasis on mood and atmosphere.

If you are interested in popular fiction genres, I recommend *Teaching and Writing Popular Fiction; Horror, Adventure, Mystery and Romance in the American Classroom* by Karen M. Hubert (published by Teachers & Writers). According to Hubert, popular genres "are legitimate forms, and they should be studied in our classrooms. By offering students the same kind of choices [for their writing] available to them in their . . . entertainment, teachers can begin to turn writing into self-entertainment."

A story can have a linear structure. For example, a story that occurs during a single day might open at 7 a.m. and move in chronological order to midnight. With strong closure, the last words could be "At least that was over with, good night"; with weak closure the end could be "He tossed and turned, wondering if the phone would ring again." Or a story can start in the middle or at the end, then flashback to the beginning and proceed in chronological order. Another alternative is to jump back and forth through time, perhaps starting the story at noon, then going back to 7 a.m., ahead to midnight, back to 10 p.m., etc. Departures from linear chronology require great narrative skill so as not to lose the reader in a time warp.

Point of view is another element to consider. Writing in the first person, or in the third person through the point of view of one character, enables the author to pull the reader into a strong identification. The omniscient point of view is less personal and less focused—both can be problems for beginning writers—but it greatly widens the range of narrative possibilities.

The movement of a story (or prose poem) depends in part on how it is broken down into sentences and paragraphs. Thomas Wolfe once followed a ninety-word sentence with two one-word sentences: "Where? When?" Sometimes a single clause (usually, but not always, an independent clause) deserves to be a sentence all by itself; and some sentences deserve their own paragraphs.

Another form students can work in is the short play. Playwrights have to tell their stories almost exclusively through dialogue and action (unless, of course, a Narrator is written into the cast). The play's equivalent of fiction's interior monologue is the soliloquy, but it is usually used sparingly. The play compensates for description by using scenery, costumes, and lighting, and also the actors' facial expressions, body movements, and vocal inflections. Writing for the theater, film, or video involves a collaboration with the actors and director, who deliver the story to the audience.

In order for a short story or play to be effective, the reader must get to know the characters and have some concern for their fate, even if it is negative concern ("I hope that guy gets his comeuppance"). The most common mistake students make when working in these forms is to be too ambitious, having an excessive number of characters and too much going on. Students who bite off more than they can write often end up dropping the work in frustration. (It sounds like that statement should be in a fortune cookie.)

Journalism. Journalism is a wide-ranging field that includes news articles, features, editorials, reviews, news analyses, and sports coverage. The term "new journalism" refers to articles that rely heavily on techniques of fiction writing, such as description, interior monologue (reconstructed from interviews), and story-like structure. Critics of the new journalism charge that objectivity gets lost in the process; proponents contend that the new journalism allows a writer to portray an event more vividly, without losing accuracy.

I heartily recommend that any students interested in writing join the school paper and write in as many forms as possible. News writing trains students to write clearly and accurately; editorials, reviews, and news analyses provide practice in essay writing; and features—particularly in the new journalism style — permit a great deal of creativity in language and structure. Newspaper writing also engenders discipline. Some writers find that their fingers entwine as the clock ticks closer to a deadline; working on the school paper may help students learn how to cope with the pressure. My own newspaper experience taught me not only to survive but sometimes even to thrive on deadline pressure, which gets my adrenalin flowing.

But more important, newspaper work developed my ability to look, listen, ask questions, and then put the results into writing.

SUBJECT MATTER

Early on in a workshop I ask students to name any subjects that would make good material for poetry and other creative writing. If the answers seem to reflect a narrow view (spring, love, extraordinary events), I then ask for subjects that are *not* appropriate. It's a trick question. If several suggestions are made, I write them on the board and add a final possibility—the correct answer—"None of the above."

Nature, love (and the lack of it), and the extraordinary will always be rich subjects, but there is so much more. Volume II of this book suggests numerous subjects for writing; what follows are discussions of three general areas that you should consider and discuss with your students at the beginning of a workshop.

The Commonplace. Common, everyday thoughts and occurrences are as worthy of the writer's attention as cosmic notions and overwhelming events. As William Carlos Williams once commented, "everything in our lives, if it's sufficiently authentic to our lives and touches us deeply enough with a certain amount of feeling, is capable of being organized into a form which can be a poem." A good detective can isolate clues where others see only a mess; similarly, a writer detects material amid the clutter of everyday life. Some do it more naturally than others, just as some newspaper reporters have a "good nose for news" and can "smell" a story cooking while others don't even pick up the scent.

A "good nose for poetry" may be partly instinctual, but it can be developed through writing and reading. One method of expanding the horizon of possibilities for your students is to make note, when you bring literary material to the group, of the subject matter. When I started reading contemporary poetry and saw that poets were writing about everyday matters, I thought, "Hey, I didn't know you were *allowed* to write about *that* stuff. Let me try it."

Beauty can be found in common places. In William Carlos Williams's poem "Between Walls," pieces of a green bottle shine among cinders. A writer need not find beauty in a commonplace object or event for it to be worthy of a poem. Williams said, "The commonest situations in the world have the essence of poetry if looked at correctly," but he added that if he wrote about "a dirty old woman in the street, it is not necessary to put her in the situation of a princess." Writers, like baseball umpires, should call them as they see them.

Wordsworth explained in the preface to his *Lyrical Ballads* that his objective "in these poems was to choose incidents and situations from common life, and to relate or describe them. . .in a selection of language really used by men, and, at the same time, to throw over them a certain colouring of imagination. . . ." Material can arise anywhere, anytime. On the way to

61

work, a writer may observe a common scene and write a three-line poem about it. Picture this:

It is early on a winter's morning, several decades ago. Charles Reznikoff and his wife are riding through the Bronx in a cab on the way to the subway, which will take them to work. As he recalled it many years later,

> looking out the window I saw in the dim light of the morning those red lights around an excavation. The sight moved me, perhaps because it was a dim morning, and the result of being moved was that I wrote this:

> About an excavation
> a flock of bright red lanterns
> has settled.

> And that's all I had to say about it.

The key word in Reznikoff's three lines, the "colouring of imagination" that dubs this observation into "poemhood" is "flock," which implicitly compares the lanterns to birds.

Upon hearing this poem, one of my students complained, "*Anyone* could have written that." My answer was, "Precisely—anyone *could have*, which is why I have hope that any of *you* can write good poems. But how many others passed that excavation site or thousands like it on that morning or thousands of other mornings without even looking out the car window? How many looked out the window and saw the lanterns, but didn't make any special notice of them? How many noted there was something eerily beautiful about them, but didn't attempt to write about it? How many did try to write about it but wound up with an overwritten treatise full of enthusiasm but devoid of impact? How many pared it down to three essential lines, which have been printed and reprinted and imprinted in the minds of thousands of readers long after the sun rose on that winter morning, long after the lanterns were removed and a building constructed? How many? Only one."

As I write this alone at my desk on an October morning, I almost hear a reader's voice, months in the future and miles away: "But what is the *point* of this 'lantern' poem?" A poem never needs to have a "point," but in fact there is one here. As a result of reading this poem, I have found myself looking more closely at excavation sites, not only to wonder what is going up, but to appreciate the wonder of what is there. It has affected the way I look at something. That's a pretty big point.

Encourage your students to write about things they might not previously have considered "worthy" as subjects for writing. Wild imagination can result in spectacular poems, but our day-to-day lives don't have so many spectacles. Some students write about far-away forests while missing the tree in the backyard or the traffic light on the corner. "Quiet" poems can be quite moving. Here is an excerpt from a fourth-grader:

> . . . looking at things I never stopped to look at before. Like my new ladder

for my bunk bed. It has a dark brown on one step and a light brown on another. And my new pillow case—I never knew it had a small pink flower right in the middle. Then when I am in the middle of my quietness I hear a key jiggling....

—Lisa Bracero

This kind of attentiveness helps students develop a feeling for details as well as a greater awareness of their surroundings, including their pets, families, houses, and neighborhoods.

MOTTO

In the dark times
Will there also be singing?
Yes, there will also be singing
About the dark times.

—Bertolt Brecht

The Dark. Brecht was writing about dark political times, but his poem can apply also to dark personal times. When my high school literary magazine came out, one of the women who worked in the lunchroom read it and asked with sincere concern, "Why do you kids write about such *depressing* things? Can't you write about happy times?"

But we students didn't find the contents of the magazine so depressing (which may or may not say something about our lives). The contributors to the magazine, who were working without the direction of a creative writing teacher, were writing what came naturally, not as a response to the assignment "Write a depressing poem." Emotional pain is a part of life, therefore a part of writing. And there is something about the adolescent sensibility (which we retain into adulthood to varying degrees) that almost thrives on a kind of "romantic" pain; at sixteen, Wordsworth wrote about "dear delicious pain..."

It is possible that writers have more of a need to write about negative experiences, feelings, and fantasies than about happy times. By writing about the dark times and the demons inside and outside of us, we experience them more fully, and they lose some of their power to wound. Plus, many writers find it *easier* to write about dark subjects; there seem to be more words and images to describe lost love, death, anger, and emotional turmoil than there are to describe joy and contentment. It's also one way of getting a break in life: If you have a bad experience and write a poem or story about it that gives both you and others satisfaction, you turn something negative into something positive.

Students should not be expected to shy away from any subject matter because it makes others uncomfortable. One eighth-grader wrote a story about his father's murder. Thinking it might have upset him to write it, I made a point of catching up with him later on. He saw me, and, before I could say anything, he said, "I want to thank you for letting me write about my father. Teachers never let me do it before; they always said, 'Oh, you

63

don't want to write about *that*.' " This was a case in which the subject matter was unpleasant, but the act of writing was satisfying. He was saying in effect, "Oh, it felt good just to talk about it."

Of course, not all subjects that *need* to be written about are unpleasant; they can also be exciting and happy, as in "I *must* tell you the most wonderful thing. . . ." Like the woman in my high school lunchroom, I get pleasure out of student poems that reflect happiness, because I like happiness—in myself and in people whom I care about. I encourage students to meet the challenge of writing about happiness in an interesting way, but I would never discourage students from "singing about the dark times."

Touchy Subjects. Some subject areas can bring up the issue of censorship. What, if anything, should students be discouraged or restrained from writing about, and what is inappropriate for publication in a school literary magazine?

Adult creative writers have the freedom to write about antisocial subjects. Novelists, poets, and screenwriters are not only *allowed* to write about things most people disapprove of in practice, but they are often *rewarded* for doing so. Murder, infidelity, cruelty, and the like abound in literature and other media.

One of the lures of creative writing is that the author can go beyond the limitations of everyday life; in writing, you can jump off a building and not get hurt. You can also punch someone in the nose and not hurt them, at least not physically. Psychological punishment, however, is quite possible to do in writing, and it would be naive to dismiss this as a motivating force. Just as authors often use their writing to pour out abundant feelings of love, sometimes they vent hostility by writing a cruel poem or story. As Byron wrote, "For what is poesy but to create from overfeeling good or ill. . .?"

Antisocial, including violent, subject matter can be an object for parental concern and the school censor's scissors. I've had students who wrote about various forms of mayhem. One principal, out of a concern as well intentioned as that of the lunchroom worker I mentioned in the previous section, asked me to keep hostile and violent references to a minimum in the students' writing and in the literary magazine because he didn't want to glorify violence or project a negative image of the school.

It is difficult to distinguish between material that fosters or glorifies violence and material that merely reflects or is an attempt to come to terms with the hostility and violence that abound in society. Even if these distinctions can be made, you still must determine what, if anything, is off limits. Can we tell students not to write what they see, feel, or invent?

In addition to antisocial material, writing teachers must sometimes contend with sexual matters. Although I feel differently about these two subjects, my views on them as subject matter are the same: Neither can be arbitrarily dismissed as inappropriate subjects for writing without damaging the value of the writing workshop.

Court opinions and public sentiment have swayed in favor of allowing writers and other artists to deal frankly with sexual matters. To what extent this attitude applies to student writers is up to each teacher. Sex. Uh oh. Visions of vigilante parents, having read their children's steamy poems, demanding to know, "What kind of assignments do you give these kids?" Although I have never assigned students to write specifically about sex, they do write about it. We talk about love and human relationships, and, if you encourage young people to write about things that concern them—including fears, confusions, and causes of wonder—some are likely to write about sexual matters. Teachers tend to be more accepting of this in secondary schools than in elementary schools. "Aren't fifth-graders too young?" a teacher asked me. Not if it's on their minds, I said.

Sexual explicitness is rarely a problem, because most students tend to censor themselves, sometimes more strictly than the teacher would. Also, most younger students are more intrigued than they are knowledgeable. This is a poem by a sixth-grader in which self-censorship is dealt with playfully:

THE GIRL (sexy)

I know this girl about 13, blue
Eyes, dark hair
With her luscious red lips
She is about 5 '0 " with measurements
24 ", 22 ", 32 "
When she walks her—oops! forget it.
Her chest—oops! almost did it again
(I'd better keep this on the level)
She is very beau . . . I mean smart
When I look at her I wilt
I would love to go on a date with her
She isn't imaginary like most people say

When I enter puberty
  Girls watch out!

P.S. Especially her
                    —Anthony Sackes

Unfortunately, this poem was censored from the literary magazine. I found this particularly distressing because Anthony had tried to be discreet, only to be censored anyway. There is a possibility that in the future he may either stay away from risky material altogether or use no discretion at all, figuring, "Why hold anything back, since it doesn't make any difference?"

Here's a poem by a high school student that deals genuinely with important emotions:

I open my eyes and see yours are closed.
Mine should be, too,
but I want to see who you
really are.
You were the first
to take of me what I wanted
someone to take.
You will be the only one,
for a while, anyway. ∖
I know what will happen if I stop
thinking of you.
It will seem less important.
This is such a small part of my head
and yet lately it has been taking up
more than its share.
I want it to take its place
among my memories
and stop taking more
than it deserves.

Each teacher should decide the boundaries of acceptable writing for his or her workshop and should discuss these boundaries and the reasons for them with the class. The best way of dealing with touchy subjects may be by having a discussion about discretion. I personally make no limitations on what students *write*, but I do believe in discretion, especially when it comes to sharing work in class and publishing it. Some things might best be written in the personal notebook and not presented to the class.

If you tell your workshop that creative writing is a wide-open field, there may be a testing period during which students will see how much they can get away with. When I suspect this is happening I call them on it. A frank and firm response is generally understood by students, and I emphasize that I treat anything written in good faith with the respect it deserves.

If a student shows me a piece of work that uses four-letter words, deals too graphically with sex, or has unkind things to say about a classmate or the principal, I try to respond to it solely on literary grounds. (This attitude has never been truly tested because I have never been presented with anything that I found to be extremely offensive.) But I might not read such a piece out loud or publish it. After encouraging students to write openly about the world as they see or imagine it, it can be awkward to tell them that what they have seen or imagined is inappropriate to share with others, but most students have accepted that the school environment puts some constraints on their freedom. Generally, these constraints should get looser as the students get older.

Touchy Subjects—Postscript

When you let the chips fall where they may, they sometimes fall into delicate areas, causing sticky situations. I was once teaching a small after-school group of junior-high school students who were quite inhibited in their writing, reluctant to deal with anything but the safest material. I told them not to worry about what I might think of them, to express themselves freely. One girl proceeded to write about the "creep sitting next to me." She did not let him see her writing, and I was convinced she was writing what was important to her at that moment. When I read the group's papers out loud, I skipped over hers, but talked to her privately after class, explaining that while I appreciated her honesty, I didn't want it to be at someone else's expense. She understood and replied that she had liked getting her feelings off her chest, but she didn't want to hurt anybody either. I can't say that she and her workshop neighbor became close friends, but I think the act of writing that piece cleared the way for her to find out that he wasn't such a creep after all.

IMAGES

"Image" is one of the words most commonly used by writers and teachers of writing. Many people consider the image to be at the heart of what is "poetic." An image can elevate writing from a mere bunch of words to something with impact and beauty, but no one is quite sure how to define it.

Field, a fine literary magazine, has invited poets to answer the following questions for a symposium on The Image: "What does 'image' mean to you, as a reader of poetry and as a working poet?. . . Is it an alternative term for 'metaphor' or 'figurative language,' or are its implications different, either broader or narrower?. . . Do you think of images in terms of kinds and categories?"

The fact that these questions have to be asked indicates that imagery is an elusive concept even for working poets. For your students, it is best to define imagery as loosely as possible, and, during the course of the workshop, periodically to point out phrases in pieces of writing and conversation (including compound words like "nightfall" and "earring") that you consider to be images. I include under the imagery "umbrella" any use of figurative language—including similes and metaphors such as "imagery umbrella"—plus any phrases, including details, that appeal to the senses, particularly the visual. (The dictionary offers "a mental picture" as a definition of image.) The phrase "rows of desks topped with overturned chairs" is an image; the context in which the image is used would determine whether it is *effective* — whether it arouses and/or usefully informs the reader.

There is a phrase that echoes wherever writing is taught, whatever the language: "Zeigen ist richtig; sagen ist verboten." "Montrez-le! Ne le dites pas!" "Owshay, on'tday elltay!" "Show, don't tell." Writing that is specific, visual, and physical is almost always more convincing, as well as more interesting to read. This does not mean that *nothing* can be told straight out. Poet James Wright ended a poem with the line, "I have wasted my life," and the directness of that line is startling and effective in context.

Some corporate executives may be able to concentrate on large concepts while leaving the details to someone else, but a writer had better not try to get away with it. "Use details that reverberate," I tell students. William Carlos Williams may have been overstating the case when he wrote, "No ideas but in things," but the fact is that "things" can be very telling.

Williams's poem "Complaint" is about a country doctor who makes a late-night housecall and spends all night with the patient. Instead of telling the reader, "I worked all night on her," Williams shows it by writing, "through the jalousies the sun / has sent one gold needle." This image is physical, visual, and informative. Later in the poem, Williams shows with one detail the doctor's gentleness with the patient: "I pick the hair from her eyes."

Painters don't have a choice, they *must* show rather than tell. If a painter wants the viewer to know that a person is sad, he/she shows it visually, perhaps with a facial expression; strength can be shown by depicting muscles, and autumn by colored leaves. A writer, on the other hand, has to resist the temptation to constantly say things like "The strong man was sad in the autumn woods."

Not *everything* should be shown; details can bog down a piece. Part of the skill in writing is not only knowing *how* to use details, but *when*. In his novel *Fifth Business*, Robertson Davies wrote, "It is not by piling up detail that I hope to achieve my picture, but by putting the emphasis where I think it belongs." A story laced with excessive details not only can make for tedious reading, but the important details might be diluted by constantly being juxtaposed with unimportant ones.

If a student writes, "He was lost; he reached into his coat pocket and took out his last coin," the reader will be as lost as the character is—if the detail of the coin's denomination is not revealed. If it's a penny, then this guy is in trouble. If it's a dime, he can at least make a phone call (unless he's in a city that charges 20¢ for pay phones, in which case the writer can exploit that fact by having the character try to make the call with a dime, only to discover that inflation has deflated his hopes). If it's a silver dollar, the man can get himself a cup of coffee before making his call. And if it's a krugerrand, then the reader is not likely to feel very sorry for him (unless the banks are closed, in which case an irony has been added). The detail of what kind of coat he's wearing could also be important: A penny in the pocket of a lush, leather coat is a different situation than a penny in the pocket of a tattered, cloth coat.

I warn my students to beware of labels that are unsubstantiated. If they say a character is bossy, sensitive, unreasonable, or kind, they must prove it. "My mother is kind," must be backed up with evidence of kind things she says and does. If the writer does this effectively, it may not even be necessary to *say* she is kind. If someone is "rich," I say let us know how he/she dresses and spends money.

This poem by a sixth-grader uses exaggeration, comparison, and detail to convey information. Read it to the class and then discuss what we "know" about the woman:

The old woman with nowhere to go
waits on the street corner
with her hair tangled
and her dress faded.
She decays in the sun
and moon
but no one helps her cross.
Her face is as pale
as a pink and white balloon,
but all the people say is, "poor thing."
In her shopping bag she carries
all her worldly possessions:
her dead canary,
eight dollars,
and her diamond wedding ring.
She decays like wood railroad tracks.
Soon a young girl about 23
comes and crosses the old woman
to the other side of the street.
"What a nice girl,"
the old woman says.
They walk together hand in hand.

—Lisa Burris

The woman's tangled hair indicates that she doesn't take care of herself. Each possession shows something: the "dead canary" shows us she is mentally unbalanced; the "eight dollars" shows us she has enough money for a couple of meals, but not enough for a place to stay; and the "diamond wedding ring" shows us that she is unwilling to let go of her past, even if pawning the ring could ease her present. The image of "wood railroad tracks" likens the woman's situation to the plight of the railroads, which were once the backbone of our transportation system but are now often left to decay. Specificity enables this poem to be read either as a vignette of a young person helping a batty old lady cross the street or as a metaphorical statement that concludes with a coming together of old and young.

In a piece called "The Principal's Office," high school student Jeannie Moran wrote:

On the door, the word *PRINCIPAL* is largely written in block printing. Behind a huge, metal desk sits a man with a grey head of hair and a wrinkle here and there. He clenches a pen and glues his eyes to the paper in front of him. A crushed paper airplane marked *The Masked Caper* sits at the edge of his desk. A small boy sits across the room with his eyes filled with hate. One hand tightly grips the arm of his chair, his other hand nervously runs through his hair.

Through the details that the author has selected to tell us, we can surmise the situation that led to this scene and can feel the tension in the room.

It takes skill to select details which convey needed information. Ezra Pound translated "The Jewel Stairs' Grievance," by the Chinese poet Rihaku, and added a note about the author's use of details:

THE JEWEL STAIRS' GRIEVANCE

The jewelled steps are already quite white with dew,
It is so late that the dew soaks my gauze stockings,
And I let down the crystal curtain
And watch the moon through the clear autumn.

NOTE: Jewel stairs, therefore a palace. Grievance, therefore there is something to complain of. Gauze stockings, therefore a court lady, not a servant who complains. Clear autumn, therefore he has no excuse on account of weather. Also she has come early, for the dew has not merely whitened the stairs, but has soaked her stockings. The poem is especially prized because she utters no direct reproach.

Specifics usually communicate more powerfully than generalizations. Nuclear fission is based on the premise that if you break certain elements down far enough they will explode. Likewise, a "large" emotional situation can be presented more explosively by breaking it down into particulars. Robert Bly's prose poem "The Dead Seal Near McClure's Beach," depicting in detail *one* seal victimized by an oil spill, is more powerful than an abstract poem about *many* seals:

THE DEAD SEAL NEAR McCLURE'S BEACH

1.

Walking north toward the point, I come on a dead seal. From a few feet away, he looks like a brown log. The body is on its back, dead only a few hours. I stand and look at him. A quiver in the dead flesh. My God he is still alive. A shock goes through me, as if a wall of my room had fallen away.

His head is arched back, the small eyes closed, the whiskers sometimes rise and fall. He is dying. This is the oil. Here on its back is the oil that heats our houses so efficiently. Wind blows fine sand back toward the ocean. The flipper near me lies folded over the stomach, looking like an unfinished arm, lightly glazed with sand at the edges. The other flipper lies half underneath. The seal's skin looks like an old overcoat, scratched here and there...by sharp mussels maybe...

I reach out and touch him. Suddenly he rears up, turns over. He gives three cries, like those from Christmas toys. He lunges toward me. I am terrified and leap back, although I know there can be no teeth in that jaw. He starts flopping toward the sea. But he falls over, on his face. He does not want to go back to the sea. He looks up at the sky, and he looks like an old lady who has lost her hair.

He puts his chin back down on the sand, arranges his flippers, and waits for me to go. I go.

2.

Today I go back to say goodbye; he's dead now. But he's not—he's a quarter of a mile farther up the shore. Today he is thinner, squatting on his stomach, head out. The ribs show more—each vertebra on the back under the coat now visible, shiny. He breathes in and out.

He raises himself up, and tucks his flippers under, as if to keep them warm. A wave comes in, touches his nose. He turns and looks at me—the eyes slanted, the crown of his head like a leather jacket. He is taking a long time to die. The whiskers white as porcupine quills, the forehead slopes, goodbye brother, die in the sound of waves, forgive us if we have killed you, long live your race, your innertube race, so uncomfortable on land, so comfortable in the sea. Be comfortable in death then, where the sand will be out of your nostrils, and you can swim in long loops through the pure death, ducking under as assassinations break above you. You don't want to be touched by me. I climb the cliff and go home the other way.

This is a little poem I wrote for my students. It uses metaphor to point out that a writer can make something big out of something small.

ATOMIC POETRY CRAFT KIT

take a molecule of vision or feeling

and cut it
    finer and finer
        until

BOOM!

Imagery and acrobatics with language are not essential for a piece to be successful. Some writing succeeds on the strength and clarity of what it has to say. Take a look at this poem by a high school student dedicated to a younger sister:

I know you're in a position you dislike.
Being the youngest is difficult.
You are forced to watch us advance
As our lives come into focus for us,
And our desires are fulfilled
While you feel you are standing still
In time, watching us pass you.

You hurt me when you say you're upset,
And don't wish to talk.
You tell me I won't understand.
Maybe I won't, but I'll always be
There to listen to you
To hug you if you want to cry.
Be patient. Money, fancy clothes, and
Discos don't make you grow any older.
Savor your childhood, think about *now*—
And smile.

—Alison Zucrow

This poem has no imagery, metaphors, or innovative use of language. But it is a clear, honest, direct communication of sincerely felt material. It's good writing.

The Image—Postscript

There's one image that seems to come up inevitably with most elementary school students. Sooner or later, they find it appropriate to incorporate a Martian into a piece of writing, often with only the barest motivation. Kids can be writing about household chores when suddenly a Martian will appear in the sink; or about school, when a Martian will show up in the principal's office. Another near inevitability is that they will find a way to spell it wrong—Marshan, Martain, Marchin, Marshin. . . .

SYMBOL AND MEANING

OSCAR WILDE: "Whenever people talk to me about the weather, I always feel certain that they mean something else."

SIGMUND FREUD(?): "Sometimes a cigar is just a cigar."

UNIDENTIFIED PROFESSOR OF LITERATURE: "*Moby Dick* is a damn good fishing story.

Few elementary school students are concerned about symbolism in their writing, or "what it all *means*." My advice to high school students regarding symbolism and meaning is: Don't go looking for them; if you are alert and sensitive, they will find you. If an object or event moves you to write, there may be something symbolic or meaningful about it.

William Carlos Williams was probably not thinking in symbolic terms when he wrote "The Red Wheelbarrow":

So much depends
upon

a red wheel
barrow

glazed with rain
water

beside the white
chickens

But a reader wrote to Williams with this analysis:

So much depends upon
The ovum and the sperm (chicken)
Man's ingenuity (wheel)
His labor (barrow)
And the elements (rain).

Writers should leave it to the critics to figure out all the symbolism; after all, we wouldn't want to put anyone out of work. If writers do insist on thinking about the symbolic nature of their own work, they should wait until the piece is finished and should carefully weigh the temptation to go back and tamper with the work in an effort to make the symbolism and meaning more consistent or clearer to the reader. In so doing, they might mess up a good thing. Wisdom in writing is not always directly proportionate to the writer's conscious efforts (some of our best symbol-making comes while we sleep). A basketball player who makes shot after shot is said to be "unconscious"; when he/she stops to think about it, the basket may seem to decrease in circumference.

We can perceive a tree as beautiful, awesome, and delicate, but not *meaning* anything beyond its presence; or, we can infer metaphorical overtones regarding the cycle of life and death and think of the roots as symbolic of the tree's unconscious. Literary works, too, can be appreciated for what they may mean, but the writer should first be concerned with making the work come to be. "Meaning" will probably come along anyway for the ride.

THE WRITER'S RIGHTS (AND WRONGS)

Poetic License. "Poetic license," a phrase bandied about in casual conversation, refers to any deviation a writer takes from the norms (i.e., from objective truth, syntax, diction, or grammar) to attain an effect not otherwise possible.

Many writers change facts for literary purposes—creative lying. A writer, in transporting a character from real life to a story, may make him graying instead of balding, a lawyer rather than a doctor, and more obnoxious—or gracious — than he actually is. A love relationship can be presented as closer, and the breakup more painful, than it was. When E. L. Doctorow was asked whether Henry Ford and J. P. Morgan had in fact met each other, as they did in his novel, *Ragtime*, Doctorow replied that *now* they had. In the first poetry workshop I participated in, led by David Ignatow, someone suggested an interesting change in a poem I had written based on

73

an actual experience. "But that's not the way it happened," I said, worrying about how the other participant in the experience would react. "What do you want, the facts or a good poem?" Ignatow asked.

Writers can not only alter facts, but they can make things happen in literature that would be unlikely or impossible in day-to-day reality. Readers often have to suspend disbelief in order to accept exaggerated situations and compressed events (something that might in actuality take weeks to transpire can happen in a story over the course of a day). Writers, in other words, create truths by not always "telling the truth."

Writers also use poetic license when they alter the syntax of a phrase or contract a word to meet the constraints of rhyme and meter. Most contemporary poets eschew rhyme and meter, so this application of poetic license is not so prevalent today, but writers sometimes use unconventional syntax to achieve a desired sound or emphasis. This line by Tomas Transtromer, translated from the Swedish by Robert Bly, has a wonderful "backward" movement:

> A Portuguese fishing boat, blue, the wake rolls back
> the Atlantic always

Writers occasionally change a word from one part of speech to another: James Joyce described a dog "almosting" a bone; and a student wrote, "I radio myself to sleep." More rarely, writers coin new words, perhaps by altering old words: poet Bill Knott's "slurprise" and "nowaminutes" (which, as a play on "nowadays" could be, in these hurried times, a useful addition to the language) from his book *Rome in Rome;* and a student's "squinching up into a ball."

Sentence run-ons and fragments are also among the devices writers use that they probably didn't learn about in school (although these things should be discussed openly in writing workshops; otherwise, students will probably pick them up "on the streets"). Generally, creative writing should not be punctuated any differently than expository writing, although for stylistic reasons unconventional uses of punctuation are less likely to occur in essays than in poems and stories. One student wrote, "I'm sorry I didn't mean to do it." According to the rules, there should be some form of punctuation after "sorry," but a stylistic effect is achieved by not using any. Another student wrote, "I ran out of my house crying, I don't want to live alone. Not a brother, not even a sister." The sentence fragment here is quite effective.

Be careful I tell students you have to know what you're doing you shouldn't just. Break rules. For the sake of breaking them as Bob Dylan sang, "to live outside the law you must be honest." Only when appropriate.

Students should be aware of the legitimate uses of poetic license, but not use it as an excuse for careless syntax, ignorant alterations of fact ("As we sat in London, the capital of France"), and grammatical errors with no redeeming literary value. In 1575, George Gascoigne wrote that poetic license allows changes that would not otherwise be "lawful or commendable." Writers should break the laws of discourse only for commendable reasons. When you don't go "by the book," your choices are unlimited; writing something that is technically incorrect or stylistically unconventional, rather than being the easy way out, requires a great deal of care.

Attempts to be "poetic" can backfire. While a shift in syntax can have a poetic effect, a writer must be careful not to obscure or even mangle the meaning in the process. The *New Yorker* magazine quotes this example from a Tallahassee newspaper of an attempt to reach for an effect that fell right on its face: "Bored? You don't have to be in Tallahassee." A less exciting but also less embarrassing way of putting the same thing would have been: "You don't have to be bored in Tallahassee."

When students deviate from the norm there can be some doubt about whether they are reaching for a literary effect or the deviations were a result of accident or ignorance. Either way, what's important is whether or not the item in question is successful. If so, make sure the student understands what happened. If not, then some revision is in order, whether or not the item is a result of poetic license or laziness.

Grammar. I hear some people bad mouth grammar. Grammar is good. I like it. Sometimes I downright love it, the way applying a rule of usage can cleanse a sentence of ambiguity. Other times I have my doubts, when grammar stubbornly insists on making distinctions that seem to have no other purpose than to confuse writers. Or when it makes something I write not sound like something I'd say. But, as with any other relationship, you have to be tolerant of little quirks, although you shouldn't blindly accept unreasonable demands. You can say this for grammar: it's willing to change, if not exactly *with* the times, then not too far behind them. If you are a true friend to grammar, you will *help* it change, but not irresponsibly.

All in all, if you have patience and are willing to accept some of the bad with the good, grammar is a great friend to have on your side. People who shun grammar sometimes are defenseless against harsh attacks by red pencils, and can find themselves being misunderstood at crucial times.

Some creative writing teachers have been perceived by other teachers as adversaries of the champions of grammar. Maybe it's because some of us speak rhapsodically about the importance of self-expression and give only lip service to adhering to the standard language code, or go so far as to advise ignoring the code whenever it is an enemy of holy creativity. Maybe it's because some of us say things like "Well, *I* don't teach *grammar*. *I* teach *creative writing*." Maybe it's because we don't seem like loyal allies of grammar, sometimes praising a student's imagery and inventiveness without saying, "Look at the vicious beating you gave to grammar; now is that any way to behave?"

Well, I think we can work it out, for I don't think a good creative writer would want to send grammar off on a one-way trip to Tierra del Fuego and be left to fend all alone in the wilds of language.

Writing teachers vary in their approaches, attitudes, and priorities regarding grammar. The study of grammar is important in providing a terminology with which to discuss writing and in informing students of the accepted language code—what is currently the standard. This code is neither more nor less than a consensus of what is correct at any given time. I was taught never to split infinitives, but "never to split infinitives" doesn't sound as good to me as "I was taught to never split infinitives" (which is a sentence not without charm). The consensus on split infinitives is shifting, from "never" to "sometimes." When I was in school, I was also told not to start a sentence with "but" or "and." But now it is quite accepted. And writers find that using these words to begin sentences adds emphasis.

In the fourteenth century, Chaucer wrote in *Troilus and Cressida*, "Ye knowe ek that in form of speeche is chaunge." If that statement were to show up on a student's paper today, a collective sigh of exasperation would fill the teacher's lounge. Translated into "correct" English, Chaucer's sentence becomes, "And then, you know, the forms of language change." You know?

Some research indicates that the formal study of grammar does not increase grammatical skills in writing. The fact that a student knows the rules does not mean he/she can apply them. Grammar should be taught in conjunction with an extensive writing and reading program. In this way, grammar will take hold and become second-nature through continuous experiences with language.

When grammar and punctuation exercises are assigned, they should be prescriptive to a student's individual problems, when possible, or apply to an area in which the class as a whole is weak. No system of exercises, no matter how well-conceived, should ever be used *instead* of writing. As Mina Shaughnessy wrote in *Errors and Expectations*, a landmark book dealing with teaching writing to remedial college students, "It is the business of a writing class to make writing more than an exercise, for only as a writer, rather than as an exerciser, can a student develop the verbal responsiveness to his own thoughts and to the demands of his reader that produces genuinely mature syntax."

As a teacher you have to make priorities. In a creative writing workshop it is important for students to write expressively, comfortably, and with self-satisfaction. It can be counterproductive to ask developing students to write expressively *and* perfectly. If we can get students writing, they will learn that most conventions of discourse aid rather than detract from self-expression, and they will be motivated to learn the conventions. Once students value their writing they will *want* it to be presentable to the public.

The more you write, the better writer you become; grammar is learned partly through practice. I tell students that if I overlook grammatical errors in their writing, it is because at that particular time grammar is on the back burner, not in the garbage can. Refinements can come later, but they should come sometime.

Since grammatical adjustments are usually made during the last stages of revision, I do not expect total correctness in pieces that students have not had the opportunity to revise fully. But when students who have the time and the capability to write correctly fail to do so because of neglect, I remind them that the reader has a tough enough job to do (and there are a lot of other writers competing for the reader's time), so it's best not to make the reader work harder because of the author's insufficient attention to grammar. At the other extreme, some students with a firm command of the language "show off" with complicated sentences that, although correct, are unnecessarily difficult to plow through. Anything that veers from the most direct means of expression should be justifiable. A writer is complimented when a reader says, "This story really makes me think," but not when the reader means, "It makes me think hard to figure out what the hell you're trying to say."

Grammar—Postscript

The word "glamour" descends from the word "grammar" and originally meant "magic" or "a spell or charm," qualities that were associated with those few who knew Latin grammar. Grammar has certainly lost much of its glamour, as students have come to equate it with tedious exercises rather than the ability to cast a spell with words.

Dialect. The question of correctness is muddied when dialect crops up, which occurs when some students write in their "natural voices," the way they speak at home or to their friends. This includes, but is not limited to, Black English. Traditionally, many groups of people have used two standards of language—one at school or on the job and another at home. As H. L. Mencken wrote in *The American Language*, "Let the daughter of a hog-sticker in the Omaha stockyards go home talking like the book and her ma will fan her fanny."

Language is not monolithic; Mencken cites the disparity between a Harvard professor and a Boston bartender. But what happens when a Boston bartender's child winds up in a Harvard professor's composition class? Some defenders of the linguistic faith wince when dialect comes out of the living room and off the street corner and lands on the written page, although they are usually more tolerant with a poem or short story than with a formal essay. If you demand of your students a more formal approach to language in essays than you do in creative writing, don't give them the impression that it is because creative writing is not as important as other kinds of writing: "It's only a poem, so it's all right." That attitude trivializes both creative writing and the students' linguistic heritages.

When students use dialect in their creative writing, you should determine if the usage is consistent and if the piece communicates effectively. If the answers to these questions are yes, then you are not in the realm of "good" vs. "bad" language, but standard-accepted and minority-accepted language. This piece of writing by a fifth-grader is not unclear: it communicates well, but not in standard English. Any revising of the language could better be called "translating" than "correcting":

> The last time I went down on 42 St. some of the ladies be standing on the corner with they high heel steppers waiting for pick up. Some of the men be deck out with they three piece suit and some be drinking and smoking joints and be falling all over the dark street and sleeping. Some be going to mens houses they don't even know but they don't care.

You as the teacher have to make the final decision as to how much leeway to allow and how to respond to a student who, as a matter of cultural identity, chooses to write outside the bounds of standard usage. One high school student complained to me that her creative writing teacher, either unaware or unaccepting of the fact that she was writing in Black English, constantly marked up her poems. She wanted to know what I thought of that? I told her that what was acceptable was between her and her English teacher in his class, but that perhaps he was acting out of a genuine concern that she be able to survive in college and other areas where Black English may not be understood or accepted. If she could prove to him that she could write standard English, I suggested, he might be able to perceive her as being bilingual. I also pointed out that the world's acceptance of the unconventional is often directly related to how good it is thought to be; if you are intentionally different, you certainly have to be consistent, but you may also have to be considerably *better* than others in order to get any positive attention.

There is certainly a need for a standard version of the language — and students limit their mobility by not knowing it. But literature, where language is traditionally pushed and stretched, is enlivened by *input* from dialects, which can flavor a piece of writing — particularly through the use of idiomatic expressions.

6

Revision

Getting everything the way you want it on one draft is akin to driving from one end of a city to another without hitting any red lights; it's possible, but happens only slightly more often than when the moon is tinted blue and business picks up at the Hades ice skate concession.

Without revision, students will wind up with a folder full of incomplete pieces, and they won't learn the full range of skills a writer needs. Writing, like a tennis serve, is not likely to be accurate or powerful unless writers know how to follow through.

My eleventh-grade English teacher was the first to tell me that "rewriting is writing"; I had thought rewriting was limited to correcting. Revision is more than a remedial step taken because errors have been made; it encompasses *any* response to what is written on the first draft, including the generation, development, and refinement of language.

Many students claim they have revised a piece when all they have done was to "fumigate" — exterminate errors. That is a worthy cause, but writing is much more than putting words on paper and proofreading. First, the work has to be defined and shaped. What exactly is the piece trying to accomplish? Sometimes writers start with blurry intentions that slowly come into focus; other times they begin with a clear idea that may or may not change drastically; and there are those occasions when they start with no more than a beginning word or phrase and wander around, sorting through arising possibilities, shedding more light on some areas while darkening others.

As the piece becomes stabilized, the writer engages in such revision activities as making sure the content is fully developed, the language is optimum, and extraneous matter is deleted. Usually, "fumigation," or proofreading for errors, is the last step.

Writers develop their own approaches to revision. Some like to plow through from beginning to end on each draft, and others prefer to revise in sections, particularly on longer pieces. Sometimes, I write the opening paragraph (or, if it's a poem, the first couple of lines) over and over until I am content, and then move quickly through the remainder of the first draft. This carefully wrought opening may undergo more revision later on or may be deleted entirely, but it gets me into a writing frame of mind. Once my first draft is done, I revise "on the page," making changes directly to the text. Then I copy the work over, incorporating the changes and making new ones that occur to me along the way. The rhythm of copying something over often results in making new changes. If I am very lucky, I am done; more likely, I repeat the process, perhaps many times.

——▬——

Mechanically, most revisions are additions, subtractions, or replacements. I offer students the following metaphor for approaching revision.

Imagine that you are the boss of a factory or company, and the words you have written are your employees. You are an extremely tough, demanding boss, but a fair one. If the workers are productive, they stay; if not, they go.

Some words get fired because they don't do their jobs well and need to be replaced, as in "The meal set before him was unappetizing." The word "unappetizing" gets the pink slip, perhaps being replaced by "greasy, with a faint odor of ammonia."

The word-boss must also recognize when to hire new workers—there is a job to be done, but no one is doing it: "There were stains on her shirt." Something is missing in this sentence. Were they "coffee stains," "wine stains," or "mud stains"? It makes a difference.

Words are let go if they are not needed—if there is no job for them to do ("The fact of the matter is. . . .") or other words are doing it better. Redundancy is often grounds for firing a word or phrase, as in "Department of Redundancy Department." Look through a piece to see if anything is said twice, and either keep the better way or fuse the two ways into a new phrase. If something is said both concretely and abstractly, keep the concrete. For example, "The tall, seven-foot man's eyes sparkled as he received the Most Valuable Player trophy; he was happy, and, raising his voice, he yelled, 'Whooppee!' " After several words are "laid off," the sentence might read, "The seven-foot man's eyes sparkled as he received the Most Valuable Player trophy and yelled, 'Whooppee!' " By saying he's seven-feet, we know he's tall. But remember that redundant means "superfluous," not "repetitive." Repetition can be quite effective: Marc Antony was not being redundant when he kept repeating that "Brutus is an honorable man," nor was Dylan Thomas when he wrote "Rage, rage against the dying of the light." Poets often begin several successive lines with the same word or phrase, a device known as "anaphora" (also used by orators and preachers).

You may be particularly fond of a phrase or sentence and be reluctant to get rid of it, especially with beginnings (after all, they were there when you opened shop); but sometimes good bosses have to be ruthless, even if they feel a painful twinge when they cross something out. To ease the pain of excision, you can put all your deleted gems into an envelope for future consideration. And remember, it is possible to actually *add* to a piece of writing by subtracting ("less is more"), and part of the ability to write is the knack of knowing what *not* to write (as good jazz musicians distinguish themselves partly by the notes they *don't* play) and what to delete. Rudyard Kipling said, "A tale from which pieces have been raked out is like a fire that has been poked. One does not know that the operation has been performed, but everyone feels the effect."

Words and phrases work in relationship to each other; a "flow" develops, and in retrospect you may notice a lovely image that breaks the flow. This image is a good worker, but it should go to work elsewhere.

Although many times you have to take a hard line, even a tough boss should be soft sometimes. Objectively, a phrase or image may seem ripe for dismissal and possible replacement, but something in your heart tells you to hold on. If you feel strongly enough, keep it, for it may add an intangible quality to the piece, perhaps contributing to a sense of authenticity.

—▪—

A revision technique that can combine eliminating and replacing words is "tightening," as in, "The piece is all finished, it just has to be *tightened*." If a writer concerns him/herself first with *what* is being said — at the expense of *how* it is being said—awkward and/or flabby constructions are to be expected.

In the first draft of a story, a student described "a big elevator it was very large. There was a big carpet it was covering the roof, the walls, and the floor. It was a burgundy color." The muddiness of these lines indicates that the author wasn't quite sure what she wanted to say until she said it. Once she saw it in writing, she tightened the lines to: "A burgundy carpet covered the roof, walls, and floor of the large elevator."

"I found a letter on a bush, a berry bush it was, it was a red berry bush," is also typical of the kind of sentence that comes up in a first draft. A little tightening transforms the sentence into "I found a letter on a red berry bush."

One technique for tightening is to find one or two words that will do the job of several. Another technique is to turn a phrase into an adjective

81

("things that are useful" contains two words that are not useful, and it could be changed to "useful things"). Sometimes, both techniques apply ("assignments that everyone must do" can become "mandatory assignments"). *Neither these nor any other techniques should be used when the ear says "no, it sounds better the other way."*

—▬—

Philip Roth's *The Ghost Writer* features a novelist who describes as his daily activity, "I turn sentences around." He writes a sentence, turns it around, has lunch, writes another sentence, then turns the two sentences around. I once wrote the first draft of a very short poem in about thirty seconds. I spent the next two hours turning the lines around. Here are three of the variations:

I am leaving you
because last night
as I nearly drowned
my life flashed before my eyes
and you weren't a part of it.

WHY I AM LEAVING YOU

Because last night
as I nearly drowned
and my life was flashing
before my eyes
you weren't there.

WHY I AM LEAVING YOU

Last night I nearly drowned
and my life flashed before my eyes,
but you weren't there.

And finally, the final version:

WHY I AM LEAVING YOU

last night I nearly drowned
my life flashed before my eyes

you weren't there

Meticulous attention contributes to the cumulative effect of making something "good reading." Revision is time-consuming. Flaubert spent five days working on one page of *Madame Bovary,* but Flaubert wasn't a fifth-grader at the time. As important as revision is, it is more important for students to have a wide variety of writing experiences than for them to mold every assignment into a highly polished piece.

I suggest that students do *some* revision on almost all their writing and that they select an occasional piece for thorough revision. Pieces of writing in need of revision are like people in need of help: you know they have problems and need your attention, but you don't have the time and energy to take care of them all; plus, there are some pieces you might not even like enough to spend a lot of time with. Sometimes I ask everyone in the workshop to select a "needy and worthy" piece from their folders and revise it.

I caution students to beware of diminishing returns: they should add life to a piece when they revise, not revise the life out of it. Learning to write includes knowing what to change and what to let remain and knowing when a piece has reached its optimal completion.

—■—

According to an article in the *New York Times,* computer programs have been developed at the Bell Laboratories to edit manuscripts for punctuation, spelling, grammar, and, that scourge of all writers, awkward construction. (How I hated *awk* written in the margins of my English papers; I wonder how it would feel to be so flogged by a computer.) A computer is no better than its human input, though, and these programs are based on such sources as Strunk and White's *Elements of Style,* a classic text on clear, unencumbered writing. The computer would call to task the phrase "bring to a conclusion" when "conclude" would do or advise that "in a very real sense" be sent off to the Home-for-Excess-Words.

If external revision techniques can be implemented in a computer program, then there must be a transferable rationale to them, a rationale that can be taught. Students can learn to be better self-editors by learning to look for the same common problems the computer is programmed to spot. Students, unlike the computer, can understand that these techniques are only guidelines and that the most important factor in writing is the human factor.

THE CONTRACT

Every piece of writing contains an implied "contract" between the writer and the reader. The writer promises to deliver some literary goods: when all is written, *something* must be accomplished, be it the telling of a complicated story, the evocation of a mood, or the presentation of a brief observation.

If you write a mystery story, you promise the reader a crime, clues, and a reasonable solution. If you write a surrealistic poem, you promise dreamlike images. A conventional short story promises character development, conflict, and plot, while an "experimental" short story promises only some movement of narration.

One step in revision is to look over a piece to see if there are any unfulfilled promises. If there are, students can remedy the situation either by developing a part that is lacking or by in effect removing a clause from the contract by deleting an undeveloped promise. For example, if a story has the sentence, "Susan was considered to be sweet by her friends, but there was a dark side, a shadow few people saw and no one could remove," then readers are going to feel cheated if at some point they don't see Susan's dark side. The author should either show Susan's dark side or remove the reference.

Students should also look for unjustified departures from what the reader has been led to expect. A piece should not change voice midway through unless there is a good reason (such as the narrator has a lobotomy, becomes educated, or changes in some other way). And, once a piece has been established as being realistic or close to it (some pieces alter reality slightly), it would be a violation of the contract for one of the characters suddenly to sprout wings and fly. A story, however, that opens with, "Captain Hero had barely landed on his rooftop and folded his wings when he heard the cry of distress," invites the reader into a fantasy.

Somewhere along the line the reader comes to know the borderlines. In the old TV series "Mr. Ed," it was perfectly acceptable for the horse to talk, but if suddenly the sofa had begun to weep, the viewer could have complained that there had been a "breach of contract." *There are exceptions:* a realistic poem may leap into surrealism, or a story may ease into the absurd, but these must be done with a steady hand.

As the writer revises, he/she should evaluate whether any changes in the terms of the contract "work." This is a subjective decision in which it is important to consider the reader's expectations; but the element of surprise (which plays on the reader's expectations) should not be discounted.

———

Writers vary as to how much they expect their readers to "work" on any given piece, but the writer/reader relationship is a partnership, which means that each must contribute something. William Carlos Williams—no surprise—made the clearest, fairest statement regarding the terms of this partnership in his poem "January Morning." (Notice the use of poetic license—a grammatical "error"—in the last line.)

> I wanted to write a poem
> that you would understand.
> For what good is it to me
> if you can't understand it?
>   But you got to try hard—

Writing is not a guessing game. A high school student started a piece with the line, "This apparatus which I once recognized as a simple piece of equipment now surrounds me with a cluster of memories." The piece went on to describe some of these memories, careful not to give away exactly what the apparatus was. "Can you guess?" the author asked me.

"Well, I suppose it's a tent," I replied, "but I think it's unfair to your partner, the reader, to be intentionally obscure. It's one thing to ignore the reader altogether—some writers don't like to think consciously about the fact that someone will be reading what they write—but you obviously have the reader very much in mind and are deliberately making the reader try to guess an essential fact necessary for the appreciation of the entire piece."

This attitude may emanate from an approach to studying literature in which the reader's job is to analyze what it is the author means but has done his/her best to keep all but the smartest and hardest working among us from figuring out. I wouldn't put my signature on such a contract.

BEGINNINGS

Starting a piece of writing, like meeting someone or starting a new job, can be both awkward and exciting. Unlike meeting someone—when first impressions can be lasting impressions — in writing one can alter or eliminate the start of a poem or story. Writers often don't anticipate what is going to happen when they start writing. They may start in one direction and decide to go somewhere else, or they may circle around a subject before coming in for a landing. Beginnings should be examined carefully with hindsight. Here's part of a poem by sixth-grader Alvin Brown that rambles before getting interesting:

WANDERING THROUGH SPACE

I met up with a spacedog
I'm trying to kill but I can't.
He roars like a lion.
I tried to kill, but I was terrified.
He was green, he had a lion fur
around his neck,
the rest of his body was like a dog.
I stood there.
Then I saw lips with two legs
and it was chased by a tube of lipstick
with two legs.
The lipstick tried to put lipstick on the lips.
The lipstick missed the lips.
The lipstick put lipstick on my lips....

The opening eight lines are not nearly as fresh as the rest of the poem, in which the imagery and sound are stronger. I suggested to Alvin that the first section diminished the poem's overall impact, and he agreed that the poem truly begins when the "lips" arrive.

Here is the beginning of a poem that began to find its mark on the fourth line, thus making the first three lines of "circling" expendable, although they were essential to the composing process:

The tunnel is dark
I can't think of anything
My mind is blank
My mind is like a dark tunnel....

A high school student wrote a poem that started with some abstract wandering through the "universe," which is quite a chunk of literary territory to bite off. About halfway down the page she reached "a path," and from then on the poem was concrete and visual. "You should stay away from the 'universe' type stuff," I said, "and stay on the paths, so both you and the reader know where you are." "But," she replied, "I had to travel through the universe until I found the path; I can always go back and cut the opening." Touché.

ENDINGS

Endings, too, should get special attention during revision. There is a "just right" moment to leave a party. If you leave too early, you feel unfulfilled, nagged by doubts that something important has been left unsaid or there was someone you should have met. But if you stay too long, you might feel dissatisfied in other ways: you had one piece of cheese and one drink too many; the conversation was strained at the end, people were repeating themselves, hanging on. You're not sure if you'd go to another party given by this person.

It is similar with a piece of writing. Students should look closely at endings to see if they have "stayed too long at the party." A frequent comment made about superfluous endings is, "That's anticlimactic," meaning that the ending breaks down what has been carefully constructed. Here are some types of counterproductive endings to look for when revising.

Denial: This ending denies what has gone on before, as in "This story was made up," or the classic, "Then I woke up and it was all a dream." I tell students who use the "dream" ending that they might just as well say, "And then I stopped writing; it was all a poem."

Editorial: The "editorial" ending says to the reader, "This is what the piece means, in case you missed it." This is an especially ill-advised ending when the message is so clear that stating it explicitly will blunt its impact. There's an Ashanti proverb that says, "When a man is coming toward you, there is no need to say, 'Come here.'" I would adapt this proverb to apply to editorial endings: "When you have gotten readers where you want them to be, there is no need to tell them where they are."

Editorial endings are also inappropriate when the meaning is open to interpretation and the author's analysis closes the reader off from making a different, and perhaps more interesting, conclusion.

Going too far: This is similar to the "editorial" ending, but here the author, instead of stating the message, lets the energy of the piece fizzle by continuing to write even though there is nothing more to say. In other cases, the writer goes too far and doesn't let the reader "participate" in the ending. Here is a short poem that should be one step shorter:

LOTUS

A fist grows in my stomach
I brace myself
Waiting for the punch
    —Gerry Pearlberg

I suggested, and Gerry agreed, that the poem would have much more punch if she let her readers discover it themselves:

LOTUS

A fist grows in my stomach
I brace myself

This also happens when people tell jokes or funny anecdotes; the teller goes one step too far and muffles the impact. For example, Henny Youngman's classic "Take my wife...please!" wouldn't be a classic if he said, "Take my wife...please take her!"

Cop out: In this kind of ending the author hasn't stayed long enough at the "party." The author may walk away prematurely from the piece, as in one fifth-grader's poem that ended: "and...what??!!/ I'm leaving this place/Goodbye!" Sometimes the author cops out by tying everything together with an artificial knot of finality. Death is often the verdict; the writer kills the "I" of the piece ("And then the Empire State Building fell on my head") or a main character ("But Johnny wouldn't have to worry about that mean teacher anymore because the Empire State Building fell on her head"). These are cases of cruel and unmotivated punishment. I might respond, "Don't be so mean! See if you can settle this thing some other way. And, of course, you don't have to *settle* it at all; maybe the purpose of this piece is to discuss the problem and not solve it. Take a break if you want and come back to it."

The all-purpose "it was just a dream" ending can also be used as a cop out ending when the author can't figure out what to do next. When I ask for more, students may respond, "There is no more, that's when I really woke up." "Go back to sleep," I tell them, "metaphorically speaking, that is. It was just getting interesting."

I previously quoted Rachel Satyabhashak's story about the planet "Lunatic" to illustrate a change in direction that occurred during the writing process. Perhaps Rachel was taken aback by the challenges inherent in this change of direction, because the first draft also contains a good example of a cop out ending: "...finally he lands on a weird planet named Lunatic. Looneys (the people on Lunatic) come to greet him. They grab him and say, 'We'll have to initiate you, zombie.' The Looneys initiate him but when that happens he zooms back to my apartment just in time for dinner." The reader deserves a look at the Looney initiation ceremony, and, instead of copping out by sending her brother home for dinner, Rachel should serve him a Looney meal. And what do these Looneys look like, anyway? With all of these questions to be answered and the bell about to ring it is understandable that Rachel reached for the cop out. I reminded her that there was always tomorrow.

Premature and pat endings often occur when students think that every piece of writing must be completed in one sitting. Class time and/or the imagination are running out and so the writer cops out. Not that cop out endings are always unimaginative. This personal favorite contains a witty image, and I would let it stand.

> I was sick and tired of this.
> I put myself on a tee,
> took a golf club
> and hit myself back to earth.

THE PROS DO IT, TOO

You might want to share with your students this excerpt from the *New Yorker* magazine's obituary for its contributor, Richard Rovere:

> Richard Rovere, who died the day after Thanksgiving, always seemed surprised to discover that a fellow-writer had filled a whole wastebasket with preliminary drafts before turning in an article. If that worked for someone else, fine, said Rovere, who was as undoctrinaire about literary habits as about most other aspects of life. What worked for him, he would say, was to write a piece directly on the typewriter in one long take. In reality, by the time he handed it in, his typewritten manuscript would often be an almost impenetrable thicket of crossed-out phrases, ballooning inserts, and tangles of handwritten amendments curling in and out of margins. Once an editor had followed the signs and picked his tortuous way through it, however, it would reveal itself as the usual Rovere marvel of clarity, simplicity, and insight—truths plucked out of an apparently hopeless muddle and put into an order that immediately seemed to be the only rational one. Rovere joined *The New Yorker* in 1944, and, besides turning out book reviews, editorial comment, and, once in a while, a short humor piece, covered the Washington scene for the magazine from December, 1948, until his death. Over and over, in odds and ends of confusing and disparate facts that were available to everyone he would somehow find a pattern and meaning that had eluded the rest of us. In time, his unshrill and unbullying judgments of people and events ofen moved into the consciousness of other Americans, including that of academic historians, as the way things had been. And although, like his manuscripts, Rovere's desk was usually a mess, being piled high with yellow-

ing press releases, tattered old letters, excerpts from the *Congressional Record*, and communications from the White House, a colleague with whom he was deep in discussion (his office door was always open, inviting company) would be startled to see him suddenly reach a thumb and forefinger into the morass and from it extract the one salient document that would prove a point: often a point made not by Rovere but by his visitor.

Richard Rovere, like so many other writers, travelled a complicated route to simplicity. The number of changes he made was testimony not to how poorly he had performed on his first draft, but to how very much he knew about writing, which enabled him to turn his first draft into "the usual Rovere marvel."

Here are examples of the revision process used by two highly regarded poets, Vladimir Mayakovsky and William Carlos Williams. Mayakovsky gives an example of revision by replacement. In writing his poem "To Sergey Esenin" (a poet who had committed suicide), Mayakovsky tried starting with the line:

You went off for ever to a world above.

This is Mayakovsky's comment on how he revised that line: "The...line is bad because the words 'for ever' don't need to be there, they're random and put in only for the metre: not only do they not help, explaining nothing, they merely get in the way. Really, what does it mean, this 'for ever'? Did anyone ever die for a trial period? Is there such a thing as death with a period return ticket?" His final version of the poem begins:

You went off,
        they say,
                to a world above.

"They say" not only keeps the rhythm Mayakovsky wanted, but also, he said, "eliminates any possible suspicions" about his belief in life after death.

William Carlos Williams relied a great deal on suggestions from his friend Louis Zukofsky, a poet and critic. The following material is adapted from an article by Neil Baldwin, who made a study of Williams's manuscripts.* I have chosen to illustrate an example of replacement, addition, and subtraction, using my "boss" metaphor for revision. What's important here is not necessarily to fully understand these revisions (that would be difficult without referring to the complete poems) but to recognize that the basic patterns of revising, whether for poems or essays, are common to all writers.

First, a case in which Zukofsky felt a word wasn't doing its job effectively. In his poem "Burning the Christmas Greens," Williams had written,

and opened fragile to my hand

---

*Baldwin, Neil, "Zukofsky, Williams, and *The Wedge:* Toward a Dynamic Convergence," in *Louis Zukofsky: Man and Poet* (Orono, Maine: International Poetry Foundation, 1979).

Zukofsky suggested that the word "fragile" be replaced, and Williams came up with a more concrete image:

and opened flower-like to my hand

"Flower-like" not only evokes fragility, but a beautiful fragility.

In another example, Zukofsky felt that there was a job which needed to be done, but no words were doing it. The draft of "The Last Turn" ended with:

the genius of a world
artless but supreme

Zukofsky felt it wasn't enough, so Williams "hired" these additional "workers":

...the genius of a world,
against which rages the fury of
our concepts, artless but supreme

In the third example, from "Three Sonnets," Williams was "featherbedding," and Zukofsky recommended some words be "fired" and not replaced.

As the eye lifts, the field
is moving—the river ruled
by an ungovernable determinant,
slowly between the stones

Zukofsky recommended, and Williams agreed, that "ruled/by an ungovernable determinant" be deleted.

As the eye lifts, the field
is moving
slowly between the stones

REVISION CHECKLIST

1. Don't think just in terms of eliminating mistakes and weaknesses, but also consider ways of *expanding* the work. "Addition by subtraction"(or "less is more" and "whittling down to the poem"), discussed earlier, is a valid notion, but we should not rule out "addition by addition."

2. Check the piece for the visual content of description and the use of concrete rather than abstract language. Are there concepts that should be supported, if not replaced, by details?

3. Look for spots where the level of the language can be elevated with imagery, including metaphor. Is there a more lively way of saying

something without violating the tone of the piece? The line "The alarm clock woke me before I was ready to get up" might be changed to "The alarm clock kicked me in the head."

4. Take hard looks at the beginning and the ending. Try reading the piece without either, and see if you lose anything. Does the piece need a new beginning in light of what has transpired during the writing process? Should it end where it does, or are there new horizons still to explore?

5. Are there any words, phrases, or entire sections that need to be eliminated, replaced, added, or moved?

6. Look for unwarranted shifts in point of view and tense, very common in early drafts. Is the piece written in the most appropriate tense? Although most narratives are written in the past tense, the present tense can inject a sense of immediacy.

7. Is each word the best possible choice? Should it be "desolate" or "barren"? Are there any words that might leave the reader wondering? Ambivalence is one thing, but ambiguity should be shunned. For example, a student who used the word "impatient" to describe a character was misunderstood by some classmates who thought she meant "irritable," although she had actually meant "eager." Similarly, another student described a street as being "dirty," when "littered" would have been more appropriate. If you are not sure you have the best word for a situation, look it up in a thesaurus and see if one of the synonyms might be better. Whenever you use a thesaurus, check definitions; and never use a thesaurus when you have an appropriate word but want a fancier one, unless there is a good stylistic reason. A thesaurus can also be helpful in finding a replacement for a word that is repeated too close to itself; but, again, check the definition to make sure you are not changing the meaning of the sentence.

8. Check for repetitive sentence structures, like starting several consecutive sentences with dependent clauses and having sentences of unvarying lengths. Check for too many sentences starting with "And then," "So," "And," or the like (unless it is being done as a rhetorical device).

9. Check for *too much* description: "A green-eyed, red-headed 32-year-old-man wearing a headband, gold necklace, ripped-up jacket, brown sweatshirt, blue jeans, sport socks, and blue jogging shoes opened the door" might tell us more than we need to know. If not, perhaps the information should be released in smaller doses.

10. Check for grammatical and punctuation errors, particularly in changes that have been made. Remember, a sentence added onto a final draft is a first draft of that sentence.

GIMMICKS

Brutality. If a piece seems to be overwritten—too long, too much imagery and description—one approach is to copy it over, editing extra harshly. Brutally remove anything in doubt. Read the two versions to see which of the deleted material warrants being reinstated.

"Losing." Once I lost a story, and after some remorse I tried to reconstruct it. Then I found the original and discovered I had improved certain parts, while weakening others. By combining the two versions, I had a final draft better than either of the others. The same thing happened to one of my students.

This accident can be formulated into an approach to revision: Before doing your final draft, put the piece away and write it again from scratch; then compare the results.

"Movie." If a narrative is too abstract, with too much telling and not enough showing, try to "see" it as a movie, and make the action unfold instead of just referring to it. Detail what an observer or participant would actually see and hear, minus such intrusive phrases as "I could see" or "One could then hear."

The author's advantage over the filmmaker is that the author can also make metaphors out of things not present, while the filmmaker is generally limited to what is there. Here is a sixth-grader's reference to an incident, followed by his revised "movie" version in which the action unfolds with the help of a "tennis" metaphor.

HELPLESS

When I was four, maybe less, I can remember when my mom and dad were fighting about moo goo gai pan. I was watching and felt helpless.

HELPLESS

"Janet, I'm home!" Dad said loudly.

"What did you bring home for supper?" Mom asked as she walked to the main entrance.

"Moo goo gai pan," Dad said, taking off his coat. Mom looked inside the bag. "What is it?" she frowned.

"How should I know?" Dad yelled.

"Well, you should know what you're eating!" Mom screamed.

From then on it was like tennis, with a scream being used as the ball. I emerged from my room with my teddy bear and blue blanket. I simply stood there doing nothing.

—Jesse Sheppard

It is usually necessary to summarize some of the action and paraphrase some dialogue, but enough should be dealt with directly to make the writing come alive.

Voice. Sometimes while doing a poetry reading, I instinctively read a line out loud slightly differently from the way it appears on the page, or I hear something "off" in the rhythm or word choice that managed to sneak undetected through the revision process. Later, I try to determine if I should make these changes permanent in the text.

Before declaring a piece finished, read it out loud, concentrating on the "sounds," and see if any changes occur to you.

TWO CLASS EXERCISES

Flab Reduction. Excerpt flabby sentences and phrases from your students' writings. Put several on the board and request suggestions for tightening them. You might want to have students attempt revisions of the samples individually and then compare their responses. Remind students to make sure that in the interest of tightening, they don't lose either meaning or literary style. Expansiveness can be appropriate; and extremely tight writing can be efficient but dull.

Collaborative Revision. Select a student first draft that has a lot of potential and make copies of it for the class. Discuss the piece with the students, pinpointing specific problems and areas that need work. Ask students to revise either the entire piece or a section, individually or in small groups. Then put together a composite revision of the piece. You should first obtain the author's permission; emphasize that you are not using the piece as an example of bad writing, but instead for its potential. Students who understand the writing process will tend not to be embarrassed by having their work used in this exercise. Here's an example of a first draft by a sixth-grader and a collaborative revision by his class. Note how some of the action referred to in the first draft actually unfolds in the revision.

THE BIG SHORTY (First Draft)

Once upon a time, there lived a man in Manhattan. This man was rather frail, and he lived in a local neighborhood. Everyone called him "The Big Shorty" because he would never defend himself, etc. One day, Leo (his name was Leo) went shopping. When he was bringing his groceries home, he met a mugger. At this particular spot, the whole block was watching a man about to jump off a skyscraper. Finally the crowd thought it boring, and turned back to their homes. Then they saw it! Leo and the mugger fistfighting over a half-gallon of milk, a few canned foods, and a *Cosmopolitan* magazine! One of the people said, "The Big Shorty can't take him on!" And then Leo knocked the mugger unconscious, grabbed his groceries, went up to the guy and said, "Talk what you know!" The crowd applauded and Leo went home.
                                                              —Tracy Grant

93

THE BIG SHORTY (Group Revision)

Although he was 6'2" tall, Leo Rogers was frail. His neighbors on the Lower East Side of Manhattan called him "The Big Shorty" because he never said anything when teenagers in the area made fun of the way he looked and dressed. Even the landlord of the rundown tenement Leo lived in would say, "Hey, Bignose, stuff a pillow in that shirt so it will fit you!"

One day as Leo was walking home from grocery shopping, he saw a man wearing an army jacket and carrying a chain come out of a dark alley. "He's starting to come my way. Oh my god I can hear my heart," Leo thought.

"Give me your groceries!" the man snarled.

Meanwhile, everyone on the street had been looking up at the roof of Leo's building, where a man was threatening to jump.

"Go on, jump," a kid yelled.

"Hey, don't listen to him, don't jump," an old lady shouted. This went on for ten minutes. The man on the roof started to laugh, and everyone realized he had never meant to jump. They turned their attention back to the street to see Leo and the mugger facing each other.

Leo's landlord yelled, "The Big Shorty can't take him on!" but Leo refused to hand over his groceries and soon he and the mugger were fighting over a half-gallon of milk, a few canned foods, and a *Cosmopolitan* magazine. Leo punched the mugger in the mouth and the mugger started to run. Leo brushed himself off, then picked up a couple of cans and put them back into the bag. He walked past his landlord without even the benefit of a cold stare, but before he went up the stairs he turned and said, "Next time, talk what you know, not what you hear."

The crowd applauded and Leo stood there smiling, in his baggy brown pants and loose tan shirt.

—Mrs. Takagi's class, P.S. 173, Manhattan

Revision—Postscript

When I look back at something I published months or years ago, faults jump out at me: awkward sentences demand to be reshaped, a word looks embarrassingly out of place and I think of a better one, an image falls flat, or a hole exists which I could now easily fill. Part of me cringes; I want to knock on the doors of everyone who has that poem or article and personally change the printed text. But then I am soothed by the part of me that points out that these realizations indicate I am a better writer *now*.

7

Feedback

RESPONDING TO WRITING

Writers often do not recognize possibilities or deficiencies in their own work that they might spot in someone else's. When errors, ambiguities, or possibilities are pointed out to them, they respond, "Of course, how could I have missed it?" Sometimes, writers know too much about what they *think* they have written to see clearly what is actually there, or they have been so absorbed in the complexity of writing that they have not been able to recognize all the potentials. Very little prose reaches print without one or more editors scouring its content, style, grammar and punctuation, and, in some cases, factual accuracy. Although poems are not formally edited, poets often seek editorial feedback before publishing.

The writer/editor relationship is essential to the professional writer, whether it occurs informally between friends (a draft of T. S. Eliot's "The Waste Land" was sprinkled with editorial suggestions made by Ezra Pound) or as part of a professional relationship ("I need a little honest help," the young Thomas Wolfe wrote in an accompanying note to the manuscript that became, with a great deal of "honest help" from Maxwell Perkins, *Look Homeward, Angel*). Editors and friends often encourage writers to take on projects, and they also offer support and suggestions throughout the writing process. A little feedback can go a long way. A friend read a small excerpt from this manuscript shortly after I had begun working on it and commented, "This is going to be great—I can't wait to read this book." That gave me greater incentive to *write* it.

Reliance on the editorial help and encouragement of others does not make T. S. Eliot, Thomas Wolfe, or (ahem) me lesser as writers. Students in writing workshops should learn the editor's role in helping writers conceive, shape, and revise their material. The teacher/student relationship should also be an editor / writer relationship, and students should avail themselves of your editorial services. Evaluating a piece of writing ("Say, this is great" or "It's okay, but you've done better") is only one aspect of feedback. Everything I discussed in the section on revision is applicable to feedback, because feedback is partly an outsider's input into the revision process (as evidenced by the Zukofsky/Williams correspondence I quoted): another person helps the writer make additions, deletions, and changes in the text.

————

Each teacher or editor develops his/her own style of presenting criticism. I have found that a gentle, slightly self-effacing attitude is generally the most effective. When you make suggestions, it's best not to take a confrontational approach, which some students will resist, thinking that accepting your criticism would be buckling under due to lack of willpower.

I tell students that I am teaching because I have had an awful lot of experience in writing and that it would be a good idea for them to pay careful attention to my suggestions and not reject any purely out of stubbornness or pride. *But*, teachers and editors can give bad advice. Often there is no absolute right or wrong, only questions of judgment. Students should understand that their writing belongs to them and that they make the ultimate decisions.

Actually, students are more likely to be too *agreeable* to suggestions than too resistant. Sometimes I look quickly at a piece of writing, under the pressure of having to deal simultaneously with up to thirty-six students, and I make a suggestion off the top of my head. The student, without considering, makes the change. When this happens, I say, "Whoa, I'm not positive about this change; why don't you mull it over for a while? Sometimes I reject my own criticism of *my own* writing." When students are told that the final decisions are up to them, changing their work becomes an active rather than passive action. Louis Zukofsky enclosed the following note to William Carlos Williams with a manuscript he had edited: "Here y'are! Don't accept the detailed criticism in the manuscript unless it verifies your own misgivings, doubts, etc."

Writing directly on the students' papers is one form of feedback. I stay away from using red ink, remembering my own student days when the worst fear was that your paper would be returned with so much red it would look like it had been mugged. In the same note to Williams, Zukofsky added, "I've written on the MS. lightly so it can be erased & you can still use the copy."

Written responses are time-consuming, and I suspect that some teachers shy away from assigning much writing because of the time it takes to correct and comment on the papers. Students are capable of understanding that you cannot always make comments and correct all errors. Their writing is more likely to improve as a result of doing a lot of writing than by receiving copious reactions on much less writing. The value of written corrections and suggestions is probably overrated; corrections can be overlooked by students, and suggestions lack the give-and-take of discussion. Therefore, much of the feedback I give is face-to-face, during the workshop.

Sometimes I collect pieces as they are written. Other times I don't collect anything for a couple of weeks, and then I ask students to hand in everything that's new. I might make brief comments on some of the papers, but I tell students not to expect comments, that the lack of a comment is no reflection on the work. I place an "X" in the upper left-hand corner of any papers that I think warrant personal discussion either because they have unexplored potential or because there are specific criticisms I want to make. (I also note any pieces that should be kept in mind for publication.) I ask students to discuss these pieces with me when we have a chance, usually while everyone is writing. Students can initiate such discussions even if there is no "X" on their paper. Offering too many suggestions can have diminishing returns; students may get discouraged either because they think they must have done a poor job to warrant all those comments or because the prospect of utilizing all the suggestions to carry the piece to its potential seems overwhelming.

I give a lot of feedback while the writing process is going on. I walk around the room, looking over students' shoulders (if they don't mind), and students come to me saying "I'm stuck" or "What do you think of this, so far?" This interim feedback is useful because students are actively engaged with the piece and are in a writing rhythm. (See Intervening in the Writing Process.) So as not to interfere with this rhythm, I try not to be a stickler for refinement, concentrating more on helping students move forward.

All reactions—written and verbal—to works-in-progress and to finished pieces should be perceived by students as helping them reach their potential as writers. You should present them in the spirit of inducing growth, rather than as scolding for past mistakes. I find that giving criticism in the first person enables me to get some points across less harshly. "I'm confused, what's going on here?" is easier for a student to swallow than "You're confused and don't tell what's going on very well" (the first may also be a more accurate statement). Such a question often elicits an explanation to which I can respond, "It might be a good idea to add that to the piece." The comment "You didn't write enough" can be translated into "That's good, but I'm greedy and want more," perhaps with a suggestion about how to proceed in giving more.

When I am teaching I hear myself saying some things repeatedly, no matter what the grade level, such as "Show, don't tell," "Details, details,

details," "Use images," "Make this grow," "Is this word (line, paragraph) necessary?," and "Does the reader know enough to care?" Sometimes I think writing teachers should be supplied with a few placards printed with some of the creative writing "slogans" they would be likely to use during a workshop. Then, whenever a certain situation arose, they could take out the appropriate placard and march around the room with it.

Fundamentals are important in any field. My junior-high school gym teacher used to tell us: "Fundamentals, you've got to know and use the fundamentals." Coaches of college and professional teams probably constantly remind their players of the same fundamentals I heard about from that gym teacher. Likewise, even the most experienced writers often have to be reminded of the fundamentals, so let the students know in advance that you will be repeating yourself during the workshop.

Be wary, though, of responses that don't take into account the particular situation. When dealing with so many papers at one time, it is easy to fall into patterns and to forget to give a response that considers the student. Some students need to be pushed harder, while others resist or withdraw when prodded too firmly; some need constant support and encouragement to motivate continued effort, while others would write even if no one saw the results. I must constantly try to stay alert to the student I am dealing with. I have, when rushed, fallen into a pattern of responding "That's good, maybe you can work a little more on it" to any piece shown to me with time remaining in the period. In one instance, the student had begun the piece during the previous session, had worked extra hard on it, and was in need— and deserving—of approval.

My standards vary according to the student. One third-grader hadn't been doing any writing; the teacher told me not to expect anything from him because he was "nonverbal." I found out that he had a rock collection and suggested he write something about it. He wrote a short poem about what would happen if he lived in a rock house, concluding that he'd have "a sore butt." For another student I might have considered this an "easy" joke, but for him it was a breakthrough with language, and I complimented him on his work. He was very proud of himself and went on to do more writing.

———

Student writing sometimes touches on an experiential or emotional extreme. When this occurs, I am particularly cautious in my response. We all know better than to lash into a poem or story based on a death in the family, but we should be equally careful when the writing is about an emotional high; abrupt negative criticism of a poem about a wonderful experience is deflating.

A group of high school students told me that the creative writing they did in their English classes tended to be bland because they didn't believe the teacher really wanted to hear what they had to say. They thought it was better for all concerned to play safe: "I write a nice little story and I get a nice grade with a little comment, like 'good writing.' The teacher doesn't have to deal with what's really going on inside me and doesn't have to worry about how to respond to such heavy stuff. I don't have to worry about what the teacher is going to think about me."

Given the bulk of writing that an energetic group of young people can turn out and the highs and lows and problems such a group experiences, this situation is understandable. The more effective you are as a teacher and the more excited the students get about writing, the more material there is to respond to. It is not just a question of reading so many papers, but also the fact that the emotional investment students put into their writing warrants more of a response than "good writing." There have been times when I was so backlogged with brimming folders that I joked with students about "throwing" a few classes, being purposely dull and uninspiring so they'd stop turning the stuff out.

There is no solution to this problem. Small groups which offer peer response are helpful. (See Group Feedback.) Beyond that, you can talk about the situation openly with your students and assure them that you do absorb as much as possible, even if the feedback they get is not as much as they deserve. Once again, it is critical for students to develop the feeling that the act of writing is a reward in itself.

Students should have the option of *not* getting feedback on a particular piece, of just sharing it for now and holding it up to scrutiny in the future, if ever. I've had a student go into a long stretch of writing, wanting only the barest feedback. It was important for him to enter into and stay in a writing "groove." Outside interference, he felt, would have stopped his forward movement. Sometimes students might not even want to *show* anyone what they are writing until they feel some distance from it. One sixth-grader was working on a story that he kept in an envelope marked "Top Secret." When he finally showed it to me, I asked him why he hadn't done so before, and he replied that he hadn't wanted anyone to suggest changes, he just wanted to "keep writing on my own." Now he was willing to entertain suggestions for revision and continuation.

Positive and Negative. All writers like to hear their work get praised. "Good" praise (by that I mean praise that's well presented), like good writing, should be specific. "Hey, that's just super" or "This is wonderful" can be said without having read the piece. It is better to say "It's just super the way you develop the characters" or "That's a wonderful image in line four." It's the same as the difference between telling someone "You look terrific" and telling them "You look terrific with your haircut and new sweater." Another advantage to making praise specific is that students will be more likely to do these good things again.

Positive reinforcement is conducive to growth, so when in doubt I give the student the benefit of the doubt. But constant praising can hold a writer back by bringing about a complacent attitude: "All I have to do is to keep on doing what I'm doing." And you would do your students a disservice if you bestowed gushing praise on everything they turned out, including "clinkers." They will either lose respect for your ability to evaluate writing or sense that you are not levelling with them. Either reaction could diminish their incentive to work hard, since they'll get praised no matter what they do.

There are those who believe it is best to reinforce the positive and ignore the negative, but in a supportive atmosphere students can benefit from negative criticism, which, although it may not be pleasant, can spur improvement.

I try to aim such criticism slightly beyond what the student has achieved on paper, but within his/her grasp. Tread lightly with criticism, but don't be afraid to step boldly when you are sure of your footing. When giving negative criticism, if possible point out another place in the same piece (or another) where the student did the same thing well. This way, the student will see what you're talking about and that he/she is capable of doing it: "You see how vague you are in line two — I can't picture that at all; but down near the end you use a detail and a metaphor to 'draw' a picture of what's happening." If this is not possible, point out something else the student has done well in the piece. Writing is a risky venture, and we should try to temper negative criticism with positive reinforcement. When Louis Zukofsky gave feedback to William Carlos Williams, he sensitively couched his suggestions in praise: "The verse is excellent. But I think it would gain if the ideas were not frequently repetitious." Or, "There is some of your finest writing here embedded in a discursive form which still doesn't form a setting. . . ."

If you can find nothing good to say about a piece, it might be appropriate to say, "This isn't very strong, but I *know* you can do better," pointing out that the piece is weak in comparison to what the student has done before and/or is capable of doing in the future. The concept of future potential is tricky, because writers often fear that their most recent piece will remain the best (if not last) thing they write, but you can assure students that improvement does come with perseverance.

Sherry Spitzer, a high school student, showed me a stack of poems, most of which were at this level:

I came to you with my love
But you just didn't care
I needed you so very much
But you just wouldn't share

I was hurt and feeling down
Just because you weren't around

I said, "Listen, you evidently have strong feelings, a desire to write, and a willingness to put in time. With those ingredients, I think you can do much better than this. I can either say to you, 'Very nice,' and you can continue to write at this level—which I don't think is very interesting—or I can be tough with you and help you to put these same feelings into poetry with a greater impact. It's up to you."

I had the sense that Sherry had never been exposed to poetry she could relate to and had never been encouraged to use more evocative language. I was right. Through her subsequent reading of contemporary poets and our discussions, she started writing different poems:

Maybe I should just disappear into the air.
Everyone is together, two pieces of soap molded into one
But me, I am one piece of soap
melting away in a pool of water.
I am standing in the center
but I'm not the center of attraction.
Maybe I should stand here
and wait. Wait forever and
ever, then I'll be noticed
and another piece of
slightly melting soap will
attach itself
then I'll be molded, but until
that time, I think I should
disappear into the air.

Trite and Sentimental. "Trite" is a trite response. I can personally attest that it is possible to get through an entire year of teaching writing workshops at all age levels without once saying to a student, "This is trite." Someone once told me of a research study which concluded that the epithet most likely to provoke a violent response was "stupid." If a similar study were to be done on which response most makes a writer want to give up, the winner would probably be "trite."

"Make it new," said Ezra Pound, but students should not be so afraid of "not making it new" that they become reluctant to write. W. H. Auden said, "Some writers confuse authenticity, which they ought always to aim at, with originality, which they should never bother about." In their quest for originality and their fear of triteness, some students avoid writing about the things most immediate to them and thus lose some of their richest material. Any determinations of originality should come *after* a piece is written. When something clichéd is written there are better ways of responding to it than dismissing it as "trite."

Many times, young writers do not know that what they are writing has been written repeatedly by others. When a student writes, "Sometimes I feel so alone it is like I'm the only one alive," it can be a sincere revelation. Whenever possible, refer to something that has been stated freshly in the same piece of writing and contrast that with the "trite" part. You could say something like, "Now, I've seen this kind of thing a lot, but this *other* phrase I've never come across in all the poems and stories I've read."

Try to redirect the feeling that went into a cliché into a fresher image. Here's a poem that's for the birds:

SOARING HIGH AND FLYING FREE

Look at the birds, flying high
up, up in the clear blue sky
soaring high and flying free

Sometimes I wish that I could be free
up, up in the clear blue sky
Do you think that it could be?
Me up there soaring just
Soaring high and flying free?

I could put together a little anthology of poems I have gotten from students using the image of birds flying free. (I wonder how free birds really are, especially when they are flying in formation; I'd like to see a student write about *that*!) "Free as a bird" has become an image so tired it no longer has the energy to fly. And yet, to many young writers, it is a fresh realization. They don't know that virtually the same image has been used by thousands of other people, so it's important to be sensitive and avoid the "trite" response. In the case of the poem above, I asked the author if she could find a more down-to-earth image: "What in your life can give *you* that feeling of soaring free?" She replied, "When my sister isn't in our bedroom with me." That image, developed into a poem, would be a much more powerful contribution to literature than another soaring bird.

Ranking right up there with "this is trite" as a criticism to avoid with students is "this is sentimental." Writing can have sentiment without lapsing into sentimentality, and I prefer that students *risk* being sentimental rather than *avoid* sentiment. Because "sentimentality" has become a prevalent criticism particularly associated with amateurish writing, there has been a backlash against sentiment among adult poets which has resulted in a lot of cold writing that shuns anything too emotional. I am not calling for a "Hallmark Cards School of Verse"—the facade of emotion with no substance—but am cautioning against tearing out the guts of a piece in an effort to avoid or excise sentimental flab. We must also remember that students *are* amateurs and that a "shlocky," sentimental piece of writing may be appropriate for a given occasion, such as a birthday poem for a parent.

In most instances, I try to help students be authentic *and* original, to write with sentiment in innovative ways. And, along the way, when I feel something is too trite or too sentimental I try to find an original way of telling the author.

Intentionality.

> Pourest thy full heart
> In profuse strains of unpremeditated art
> —From "To A Skylark" by Percy Bysshe Shelley

Sometimes, what people find enticing about student writing is more a result of happenstance than intention. But need it be intentional for it to be artistic? Is "Little Billy didn't realize what he was writing" a refutation of the worthiness of what little Billy has written? Many adult writers and artists don't realize what they have done either until the critics tell them.

The artistry, calculated or not, of students' work should be pointed out to them. I often read a student's poem to the class and then give a brief exegesis, usually to the delight and surprise of the author, who responds, "*I* did all *that*?" In this way, students learn to recognize the qualities which make something artistic and perhaps also how to replicate those qualities. More important, they may come to trust and treasure the instincts and senses that bring about such jewels.

Perhaps the loss of trust in one's instinctual ability to make art is why many teenagers and adults have more difficulty than young children in tapping their creativity. This is not to say that the development of creativity in older students is merely a shedding of defenses, although that is a part of it. Childlike spontaneity, if it doesn't mature and develop, can produce repetitious and formless works. While it may be true that the typical child is more open toward creative expression than the typical adult, virtually all professional artists produce better work as adults than they did as children, for they learn a lot about how to deal with their innate talents.

Sometimes an artistic moment in writing can come from an out-and-out mistake, even a typo, though it takes talent to recognize it. W. H. Auden typed "*ports* have names for the sea" in his poem "Journey to Iceland" when he meant to type "*poets* have names for the sea." He kept the typo. Although most students don't type, I have seen them make similar fortuitous errors. A sixth-grader wrote "slipper fingers," which I thought was a charming image to convey a soft touch. When I read it to the class, she told me that she had meant to write "slipper*y* fingers." I pointed out that even though it was a mistake, she had stumbled across a nice image and might want to keep it or use it elsewhere.

Purpose. The training of professional writers is not the purpose of a school writing workshop any more than the training of professional scientists, historians, mathematicians, or athletes is the purpose of other courses. Not many students will become professional writers or risk subjecting their work to the often harsh judgments of editors and critics. We are accomplishing a lot for most students if we help them feel more comfortable and competent with writing, find a place for writing in their private lives (journals, poems, letters, etc.), and become more aware and appreciative of what writers do. Their only publication may be in a student magazine, but as poet/teacher Ron Padgett says, they will learn that "if they can do it, then others who write printed words are just people, too. It's harder for them to be bullied by printed words."

When students are interested, I discuss the life of a professional writer: publishing, rejections, income, rejections, fame, rejections, satisfactions, and rejections. When a high school student expresses interest in eventually writing for publication, I may be tougher with my criticism, after making sure the student wants this extra scrutiny. But even those few students who intend to go on to become writers should not become overly concerned with the literary merits of what they write. Students should be more concerned with *writing* than with *what* they write. Neither students nor their teachers should be unduly concerned about the quality of the products. I am more interested in the process of writing than in generating products; my students need not even pursue every piece to completion. But I find that when I emphasize process, the products come naturally, proving that sometimes there *is* justice. Some writing experiences don't result in good products immediately but are part of an ongoing growth that pays dividends in future writing.

Conferences. In the middle of the term, I try to have individual conferences with students. I go through their folders, make comments, and offer suggestions based on their overall output. Going through a folder, you might notice a pattern that was not discernible when you read the pieces individually, in the midst of everyone else's papers. I also glance through rough drafts, looking out for good things that got edited out during the revision process. This is one of the reasons I tell students to keep all their drafts — sometimes they change or excise what is most daring or exciting about their writing because in retrospect it looks "strange" or "silly" to them. During the conference, I also like to hear what students have to say about their own writing, as well as questions or comments about the workshop.

Responding to Writing—Postscript

The bell rings, and a dozen papers are thrust into my face, accompanied by several urgent please to "Read this, oh, please read it." Sometimes I am late for the next class, I have already read too much in too short a time, and the best I can do is say, "I'll read them *all. Later.*"

But, if it's possible I will read a paper right away when it seems important to the student. Often, a reading is all a student is asking for, not detailed, incisive criticism. After reading a piece hurriedly, I might smile and say, "I like it" or "You've got some good stuff here"; the student may ask skeptically, "You read the *whole thing?*" So then I quote a line or an image from

memory, and the student smiles back and says, "You sure read *fast!*"
It's the least I can do.

INTERVENING IN THE WRITING PROCESS

One of the nicest moments in teaching writing is when you say just the right thing to a student, and he/she thinks for a moment, smiles, and dives back into the paper, writing energetically. This knack of saying the right thing to a student derives in part from knowing how to proceed with your own writing. I cannot overstress the importance of teachers having their own writing experiences, from doing some of their own assignments, keeping a notebook, forming a writing workshop with colleagues, or just sitting down occasionally to write. There are no great secrets to writing that cannot be uncovered in the doing.

Sometimes the most effective feedback to give students who are trying to get their minds unclogged is a sense of commiseration: "I know, I *know*, the same thing happened to me last night. It's really frustrating. What I did to get going again was to. . . ." Before you go any further, though, you should check to see if the student is ready to resume writing. Once, I got carried away with my own story while the student was writing up a storm, probably thinking, "Yeah, it can be tough, but let me get some work done."

The following three sections explore techniques you can use to help students advance their writing by intervening in the writing process. We have to remember that there is a fine line between intervening on the student's behalf and interfering with his/her writing. Make sure the student *wants* your help. Also, it would be interfering to intervene constantly; students should have experiences fending for themselves, so they can make their own discoveries. The purpose of intervention is not to help students turn out better products, but to give them insights into the writing process, which they can internalize and use eventually on their own. *Therefore, the extent to which you intervene should gradually diminish as the term progresses.*

Finding the Handle. Sometimes students have a hard time shaping their material. They know what they want to write about but they don't know how to go about it. I can sympathize with this problem; I, too, often carry potential material around with me for days or weeks before I find the handle that enables me to structure the material into a poem or story. After a particularly frustrating session, a high school student handed in the following explanation:

> The reason why I'm not writing is that some people just can't put their ideas into words. I'm one of those people. I have a good idea that I can't write about. The idea is that there is a relationship between two people and the rela-

tionship is very strong and then one of the people has to move away. This
leaves the other person very sad and depressed. The person that didn't move
away still wants the relationship to go on but the other person is too far away.

The job seems overwhelming to this student, but he can be shown that he
has the material and the strong feelings with which to do meaningful
writing. Sometimes a person has all the ingredients but doesn't know how
to cook with them. The following recipe can make the task manageable.

1. Write a section about the moment of saying goodbye: include details,
   conversation, and a description of the car driving away (or the plane
   taking off), perhaps adding a simile to the description.

2. Flashback to the time the two people met, again with details.

3. Jump ahead to sketches of the relationship growing, including at least
   one rough spot to show these people are "real."

4. Write about the moment when the news was told that one of the
   friends was moving, including the setting; perhaps there could be
   some contrast if, for example, this occurred at the circus.

5. Jump ahead to the moment *after* the friend leaves (picking up the
   story from the opening section).

This is the vignette approach, which consists of a series of related sketches
rather than a continuous narrative.

If a recipe is too ambitious, I can offer a more limited alternative. I
always encourage students to deviate from my "recipe" if they evolve alternatives in the writing.

When students are not writing, you can ask them to write *about* the
subject they would like to be writing about, to help them in case they are
having trouble finding the handle. Here is another example of a student
having difficulty moving from conception to implementation:

> Once there was a very bad feeling I had about someone. I probed my mind
> for days trying to put it into words. It was like this person cared but didn't
> care. We would talk but no interest was added. It was like a cold feeling. A
> song explained it perfectly. It was a feeling that was cold as ice.

Even though the image "cold as ice" is a cliché, at least the student has
begun to express the situation in imagistic terms. The next step would be for
the student to try to reproduce the conversation in which "no interest was
added." It hadn't occurred to him to use the actual experience, to present it
so that the reader would reach the same conclusion ("bad feelings" that
are "cold as ice") that he had, perhaps amplifying the experience with other
similes. Since one of the skills of the writer is to convey experience more
rapidly than it would take to occur, it would probably be necessary to
distill, and perhaps alter, the conversation.

Students can try to find the handle by writing out the material at random;

sometimes an appropriate form will "declare itself." In one instance, the lack of form became the form. A fifth-grader was struggling with an empty page, and I asked him if he was having trouble deciding what to write. He replied that his head was full of ideas, but he couldn't figure out "how to organize them into a poem."

"Get it down," I told him, "in notes, fragments, whatever, and then deal with organization. Make a list of what you want to incorporate into the poem." As it turned out, he liked the way his list of fragments turned out and, with a little refinement, let the poem stay in that form. When it was read out loud, another student admired the structure.

Another aspect of finding the handle is to determine what literary "angle" to use for the subject matter. Using the situation of a close friend leaving town as an example, here are two alternatives to dealing directly with all or part of the situation.

Allegorical Approach: Write about something that, on the surface, is unrelated, but acts as a metaphor for the situation, such as birds migrating.

Surrealistic Approach: The rules of reality are suspended in surrealism. For this situation, a miniature train could pull up at the breakfast table and take the person away while a faint voice yelled "All aboard!" as the person shrank into the train.

Questions. The novelist Davis Grubb (*Night of the Hunter*) would sometimes stop by his neighbor's apartment late at night, agitated after a flurry of writing, and say, "I don't know what happens next."

The question implicit each time a writer pauses is "What happens next?" The writer can zero in on the answer by making the question more specific: "What can happen to bring the father and son closer together (or push them further apart)?" "Should the phone ring with some bad (good) news?" "What association does this last line evoke?"

Writing is at the best of times a natural process, with the author constantly answering such questions without actually formulating them. But sometimes, when I am stuck, I read over what I have written to see what questions are suggested by the material. The more one writes, the more one can recognize the possibilities—where one can "go" with a certain piece of writing. Student writers may not have the experience to recognize the potentials suggested by their material, and providing them with stimulating questions can be a valuable form of feedback.

When a student asks me to look at a piece of writing, saying, "I'm having trouble" or giving me a premature "I'm finished," I read the piece and, rather than telling the student what to write next, ask out loud some of the questions I might ask myself if I were the author. These can be questions for *advancing* the text (plot and character development; association and movement of language) or questions regarding the focus and depth of what has already been written (is anything missing or underdeveloped?). I am constantly on the lookout for unexplored possibilities. Sometimes students will leave an opening you could drive a typewriter through, but they don't even recognize their own invitation.

A sixth-grader wrote a short piece using the persona of a man alone on a beach late at night. The man makes a fire and says, "I stare into the fire with wild eyes and I get a tingle down my back and suddenly I feel...like I am wasting my life away." This extraordinary realization was not followed up in the piece, so I pointed it out to the author and asked, "How did this realization affect his life?" The student resumed writing, adding that the man goes for a run on the beach, sells his house, and starts to live on the beach.

A high school student was writing a lackluster piece about a football game. There was no focus, so I asked, "Is this a sandlot game or a formal team? What does it feel like to have your face pushed in the dirt? What's the weather like? Is the field muddy?" For depth I asked, "Is there someone special watching the game, like the quarterback's father, whom he hasn't seen in five years, or his ex-girlfriend, sitting with the sports editor of the newspaper? Does he have an injury he's been covering up? What did he dream the night before?"

Another student was writing a "bum in the gutter" poem. To help him avoid being superficial I asked, "Who is this bum? Does he have a family? Was he always a bum? What is his life really like: What were the last three meals he ate? Where did he sleep last night? What does he think about himself and the people passing by who pause to scorn or pity him or write poems about him?"

A fifth-grader had written in a poem, "I am a genius. I can answer any questions." Mischievously I asked her, "What was the most difficult question you've been asked...and how did you answer?" The look on her face was not one of gratitude; I had complicated her life for the few remaining minutes in the period. But sometimes a writing teacher must sacrifice popularity for art.

Questions can help students develop imagery. A student wrote, "Excitement spreads from person to person." Question: "Spreads like what?" If the answer is "like peanut butter, " you might want to find out on what kind of bread; it does make a difference for how easily it spreads. If a student writes: "It was a nice house," ask how it was nice. If he/she answers, "because it had soft carpets," the reader can experience more tangibly some of this "niceness." You might want to go one step further and ask, "How would it feel to walk on those carpets?"

This kind of "pushing" should not go too far, lest it get discouraging. Also, emphasize that students need not answer all of your questions, but that you want them to become familiar with the process of developing their material until it becomes a natural part of their writing and they themselves sense how to recognize and capitalize on the potentials inherent in what they write. I often read a few papers out loud to the class, asking after each one a number of questions the author could consider in revising or expanding the piece.

As they internalize the questioning process, some students can almost lip sync the questions with me, an indication that they are needing me not quite as much as they used to. For a writing teacher, it's a wonderful feeling not to be needed. Until that happens, the students get used to my constant "cross-examination." When one fifth-grader came up to me and said, "Here, it's done," I responded typically by asking her a few questions suggested by the piece. She walked off in a mock huff, saying, "I knew it—he always wants *more*." The next time, to see how she would react, I read her poem and said, "Looks done to me." She was disappointed: "Don't you like it?"

———

"What do you know?" is often an appropriate question to ask students.

The teasing, singsong expression, "*I* know something *you* don't know" indicates that the taunter has something the tauntee should covet. It generally gets repeated until the tauntee begs for the information, at which point the taunter may or may not share the goods. Writers should have a more generous attitude: "*I* know something *you* don't know...and if you read this, you'll know it, too."

Students should constantly ask themselves, "What do I know that the reader doesn't?" Then they should be selective in deciding from among that material what the reader *should* know. For example, if I am writing about driving down the highway, perhaps the reader should know something of the scenery, but I would make it a dull trip if I told the reader *everything* I saw through the window.

One high school student was writing a story about a ballerina. It was unconvincing, yet the student had taken ballet lessons for years and was able to convince me verbally that she knew a lot about the subject. I said, "Ah, *you* know something *I* don't know. Maybe you assume that I know it, but I don't. Or maybe you're too lazy to tell it, or it's second-nature to you so it doesn't even occur to you to write it down. Don't overdo it — use just enough details to convince the reader this could have happened, enough to flavor the piece with the experience of dancing, without overseasoning and making it hard to digest."

A fifth-grader named Patty wrote the following poem:

Dogs are soft and shaggy
look like Lassie
And look so sassy
Pat them on the head
then go to bed

The poem has no authenticity; if Patty knew anything about dogs, she certainly wasn't sharing it with the reader. Rhyming made it even more difficult for her to really say anything. When I asked her if she knew any collies, she said no. Did she know *any* dogs? Yes, her grandmother had one. I suggested that instead of writing about "dogs," she write about a specific dog — her grandmother's — whom she knows.

Patty utilized one of the privileges entitled her by poetic license and wrote as if the dog were her own:

Some dogs are shaggy,
My dog is a chihuahua
And he eats my cat's food,
Instead of dog food.
His body is white with a brown stripe.
He has a face like a baby,
Legs like pens,
And a body like a peanut.

The first line was derived from the original draft; it served the function of getting the second version started and could be disposed of during subsequent revision. This is by no means an outstanding poem, but it is a big improvement, including details and similes. More important, Patty realized she could draw on her own knowledge and experience, making alterations to serve her literary interests.

Students usually know a lot more than they let on in their writing and should share the wealth of their knowledge. If a student says that he/she really doesn't know any more than what's on the paper — and it's not enough — then I say: Be a "con artist" and try to convince me anyway. Speculate; perhaps do a little research. Mentally project yourself into the situation and go by your instincts as to what it would be like. Yip Harburg wrote the lyrics to "April in Paris" without ever having been there (nor, as he pointed out, had he ever been "Over the Rainbow," a song he also wrote).

Turns and Twists. When a student is stuck, it may be possible to pinpoint the turn of language that put the piece in a blind alley. One student was writing a poem about nighttime, with several good darkness images. Just as the piece was picking up momentum, the "sun rose." "Slow down time," I suggested. "Let the night last a little longer."

In other cases, the poem or story needs a "twist" of some sort, and you may be able to point out where a monkey wrench could be thrown into the works to make a more interesting situation. In fiction, especially, roadblocks and detours can make a story more interesting than just having the characters ride along smoothly. One student was writing a story about a poor child and his aunt living in an underdeveloped country. They were starving and got arrested for stealing bread. It was a typical story about oppression and hunger leading to an understandable crime, leading to a typical ending: the two were sentenced to twenty years in jail. I suggested that the best challenge to these characters (and the author) would be not to have the judge sentence them to twenty years in jail (which is what they expected and where they would get fed) but to have him say in a whimsical mood, "I'm bored with these cases; sentence suspended, you're free to go." This ironically sadistic sentence would put the characters right back on the streets with the same problems. How would they react? What would they do to turn their lives around? A story that had been over would now be just getting interesting.

Intervening—Postscript

When I was writing for a newspaper, I found out that sometimes it's helpful to intervene by recommending that someone *stop* the writing process. I was working on a feature, and it kept growing and changing; whenever I thought it was done, I realized there were still unexplored possibilities. The deadline arrived, and I said, "I need more time." A week later, my editor came over to my desk and said, "Look, eventually you just have to stop, and go on to something else." From time to time, as I refuse to let go of a piece of writing, I hear that editor's voice. Sometimes, when I am working with a student, I hear myself saying it, too.

GROUP FEEDBACK

Writing workshops on the college and postgraduate levels usually consist mainly of the participants bringing in work for consideration by the group. Sometimes the writing is copied and distributed to workshop members in advance. The author reads his/her piece aloud, and discussion ensues, with workshop members offering reactions and suggestions. The instructor's involvement—including assignments and class exercises—varies according to personal style. Peter Elbow, in his book *Writing Without Teachers*, proposes that workshops can function productively without an instructor. Some of your students, especially at the high school level, might want to form such a workshop, which would meet outside of class.

Group criticism should be part of the classroom workshop at any grade level, so that students can get feedback from each other. Involving the students in the feedback process greatly increases the amount and range of responses. It also takes the burden off the teacher to be the sole responder to every piece of writing, as well as the sole authority on questions of literary judgment.

The class can be divided into groups of 4-6, and you can have several feedback sessions going on simultaneously. (A group could spontaneously decide to have a session while others are writing, with the stipulation that members not be coerced to join the session if they would prefer to work on their own.) You can roam from group to group, and each group can elect a "managing editor" to keep things moving when you aren't there.

A discussion about the dynamics of these small groups should take place before you start, and you should have follow-up discussions a couple of times during the year. One point you especially need to discuss is the common reluctance to criticize someone's writing either because of fear that he/she will "get even" when you read your own work (whereas compliments are more likely to beget compliments) or because you don't want to hurt his/her feelings (so you are overly "polite" in your comments). Point out that criticism should be given and taken in the spirit of helping and that it may not help a writer to hear nothing but compliments. Students may at first feel uncomfortable about criticizing their peers and putting their work on the line; many writers never feel at ease with this situation. But eventually a group identity forms as the participants get to know and trust each other and become familiar with the various ways of responding to writing.

Perhaps the two most common responses to a piece of writing that I have heard in workshops are "It works" and, you guessed it, "It doesn't work." Depending on the degree of temerity or sensitivity of the critic, these phrases may be followed by "for me." Sometimes these are appropriate responses and much better than conjuring up pretentious reasons when you really don't know *why* you like or dislike something. (Other times, they are non-responses, perhaps meaning "I really wasn't paying attention" or "I'm totally baffled.") Critics should not feel obligated always to have something to say, to show how "smart" they are. An offhand remark, uttered for the sake of participation, can be taken quite seriously by the recipient.

Because writers are often insecure about their work and have the desire to be understood and appreciated, it is difficult for an author to avoid jumping into the discussion of his/her own piece. But it is beneficial for writers first to get feedback based only on what is actually written on the page. When an author publishes a poem or story, he/she is not available to each reader to answer questions and elaborate; the text must stand on its own.

Therefore, I recommend that the author not make comments or answer questions during the first part of the discussion. If I ask the group, "Do you think that this phrase is meant to be funny?" and the author bursts out, "Yes, that was a joke," then he/she may be deprived of finding out if the readers picked up the humor. The author should listen attentively to see what effects the work has wrought in others. After the group has made comments and responded to questions I have posed, I ask the author if he/she wants to *ask* any questions of the group, such as "I'm not sure about the image in line three—does it sound too corny?" or "Does it come across that the father is being insincere?" *Then*, the author can answer questions and/or make comments he/she has been suppressing.

I tell students there should be a salt shaker at every workshop so that a grain can be placed on each comment. I want them to understand that taking criticism (positive or negative) too seriously can be as harmful as ignoring it categorically. The smartest and most well-intentioned critics can be wrong.

REMEDIAL STUDENTS

It is painful to read a badly botched piece of writing, particularly when you know the student really tried. Teaching remedial writing has become a crucial focus in education, one which affects all teachers: poor writers have a hard time succeeding not only in English but also in social studies, science, and other courses. Writing problems get passed upward; I've had advanced composition students in college who could not write fluently.

Students who fall below grade level in reading and writing are in a perpetually precarious position. Unless something happens to turn around their lack of progress, they are faced with both the difficulty of learning these skills and the isolation of being behind their peers. The further up the educational ladder they go, the weaker their foothold becomes. Anything you can do to get these students writing is a step in the right direction, for it helps break down the barrier between them and written expression.

I've noticed a certain kind of discipline problem among some remedial students, especially in the upper elementary grades: "good kids" who are friendly to me in the halls become monsters during class. They are so intimidated by writing and feel so helpless that they'll do almost anything to avoid confrontation with the blank page, often putting it off until there is so little time left in the period that not much can then be expected of them. They finally begin to write, and the bell rings.

Since many remedial students feel defeated before they begin — the job seems too enormous — I try to find tasks they can handle. It doesn't matter how small or seemingly inconsequential these tasks are, as long as they lessen the students' fear of writing.

My assignments for groups of remedial students are generally not fundamentally different from what I give other classes, but I break them down into smaller units, to make them more manageable. The students take things one step at a time. For example, in an assignment to write a profile of a person, I might ask first for a physical description (clothes, hair, eyes, etc.), then for a couple of sentences about the person's job, about the family, and perhaps about a dream the person might have had. The result may be complex, but the process is simplified.

Sometimes I ask a student merely to list anything he/she has seen or thought about in the last day or two, including anything that happens while they are writing. Here is a typical list:

I saw my sister in the bed last night when she was sleeping.
A lady just walked in the door.
My mother told me to go to the store.
That man is drinking water.
The lady brought some drawing paper into the class.
My sister is down south.
Last night it was raining.
It is sunny outside.

The next step is for the student to expand on as many of the statements as he/she wants to, by adding adjectives and adverbs or by extending the sentence with an additional clause. This process is best explained to the student by example rather than by using such words as "adjective" and "clause." The above sample becomes:

I saw my sister in the bed last night when she was sleeping. *She was curled up like a snake.*

My mother told me to go to the *grocery* store *to get a quart of milk and a loaf of whole wheat bread.*

My *older* sister is down south *in college.*

The process of expansion can go on from here, with each of the original sentences serving as the seed for developing a full paragraph.

It can be useful for remedial students who speak English as a second language or who speak Black English or any other dialect to use these "voices" in their creative writing. Students can then translate these results into standard English and see if anything is lost in the translation. The idea is for them to become more comfortable with writing, which can happen faster when they are able to utilize language they are more in control of.

In studying papers by remedial college students, Mina Shaughnessy discerned patterns in the writing: certain errors appeared in predictable ways, often directly related to the students' linguistic backgrounds. This is important because when these patterns are understood, part of the student's job becomes to learn a new "code" rather than to start from scratch. According to Shaughnessy, if the teacher is to be of use in this process, he/she "is in the position, first, of having to teach features of English he has seldom had to think about, features whose complexity and irregularity or arbitrariness have been masked by habit, and second, of having to search out the logic of his students' preferences for erroneous forms."

A remedial student should be dealt with with respect for both the person and the writing. Ask yourself: What is he/she trying to communicate, and what has gone wrong? If you can understand what the student is attempting to say, then you will have an easier job of explaining how it should be said. Assume that he/she *is* trying to say something; if it's not clear by reading the paper what that is, then ask. The discrepancy between what's on the page and what was on the student's mind can be enormous, and the only way you can help bridge that gap is by dealing with both.

Look carefully at "illiterate" writing; don't just cast it off as hopeless — you can pick up from where the student is.

Encouraging Second Drafts. Here is a first draft by a remedial elementary school student:

My grandmother was nervous she had her glasses upsaiddown a smoking the cigarette the rong way I know she was nervous. she had her shoes on backward they was black shoes her hair was stand on her haed.

114

Obviously, this student has problems, but the situation is not unworkable. She had help with some of the spelling, and the misspellings, like "haed" and "rong," are good attempts to spell words the way she pronounces them; they are close enough to the correct spelling that we know what she is trying to say. She has grasped the basic thrust of the assignment, which was to use details to communicate emotions. This paragraph shows that she writes as the ideas come to her, with little pre-sorting, which is common even in first drafts by advanced writers. (But she had probably never gone beyond a first draft.) First, she decided to say her grandmother had her shoes on backwards, then added the information that they were black shoes. This could easily be revised: "She had her black shoes on backwards." In subsequent drafts, the student was encouraged to explore *why* her grandmother was nervous, as well as what else she said and did as a result. These are not insurmountable tasks; the foundation is there to build upon. Remember, this paragraph is only the starting point, where work begins, not the final product of a hopeless student.

Trying to tell the whole story in one swoop is a common pitfall of remedial writers, as can be seen in this first draft:

> This man and this lady was so poor they didn't have a peace of crumb so they met in the hallway. So the man got his shot gun. The man said, "This hurt you more than me, bang."

These few lines, which took the student twenty minutes to write, leave out the meat of the story. But he does have a story to tell. My response to a piece like this would be very encouraging: "Well, you don't have to worry about what your story is about — all you have to do is fill it in. You have the skeleton; now put some flesh and muscle on it. Take your time, think about who these people are and where they live." Don't, however, overwhelm such a student with how much needs to be done; take it one step at a time. The size of that step—the amount that can be done in each interval—will depend on the student's capabilities. One student I gave no more than a nibble at a time. She would write a line and show it to me, and I would ask a question which led to the next line. It got to be a game with her, and she was excited to receive such close attention. I gradually increased the amounts I gave her — "Now, write *two* lines before you come back." Eventually, I hardly saw her at all during class.

From Spoken to Written Language. In working with remedial students it is sometimes useful to take dictation. Many poor writers are good storytellers; but although they can tell stories verbally, they cannot transcribe these stories onto paper. With one such student, I wrote down a story as he told it, and when I showed him the results he replied, "*I* wrote that?"

I answered, "No, but you are *capable* of writing it."

Giving dictation (or speaking into a tape recorder) cannot replace the act of putting words down on paper. Dictation is useful, but students should be weaned from it. Dictation can build up confidence, but that confidence should be channeled into coping with the act of writing, which requires one to think in sync with the mechanical process of using letters to make words and words and punctuation marks to make sentences, so that the result makes sense. When you do take dictation, the student should watch the words as you write them down, and then copy over the piece him/herself. This helps bridge the gap between verbal and written communication.

A good exercise for helping students make the leap from spoken to written language is to ask them to write down jokes they often tell. This exercise enables them to concentrate on the mechanics of writing while absorbing a sense of syntax and structure (a good joke is well constructed). After the student has transcribed the joke, ask him/her to tell it to the class twice: first without referring to the paper, and then by reading exactly what is on the paper. Point out anything that got lost or changed in the process of writing out the joke.

— ▬ —

Don't judge the progress of remedial students by the number of mistakes they make. I have had students who, at the beginning of a workshop, were so afraid of making mistakes that they wouldn't try to do more than a few simple sentences, no matter what the assignment was. As they get more excited and less inhibited about their writing, they try more things—and make more errors. But there is a much more solid base upon which to confront these errors once they are writing.

I try not to forget how difficult the simplest writing tasks are for remedial students. I think about how I feel when I'm trying to learn a dance step or a difficult chord progression on the guitar or when I am overwhelmed by what I am trying to write. In the early stages of writing this book, as I was getting an idea of what the book could look like in the end, no matter how much I accomplished in a day I hardly seemed to make a dent. I then went through a period of being so overwhelmed by the big picture that I couldn't follow my own advice and break it down into manageable units. I would sit at the typewriter and, with so many things to do, find it hard to do *any* of them. I wanted it to happen all at once, and when, of course, it didn't, I had some anxious moments that it was just too much for me.

When I am working with a remedial student who is struggling over a paragraph, I remember that he/she probably feels the same way I did in those moments.

THERAPY AND BEYOND

When the question arises, "I like what these kids are doing, but is it literature?" I sometimes reply, "Who cares, as long as you like it?" The fact is I do care about literature, but not everything students write should be judged for its literary value; I am also concerned with the personal value of certain writing experiences. I hesitate to call this value "therapy," for although "poetry therapy" is seriously practiced by professionals, I am wary that the pop psychology movement will move in. (I can see the books now: *The Therapeutic Poetry Workshop: My Poems Are Me*, and an assertiveness book, *My Poems Are Wonderful, Yours Are Rejects*.) But it is a fact that writing is a means for people to get in touch with and express their emotional and fantasy lives, and that has a therapeutic value.

One value is in the release of troubling feelings and thoughts, what psychologists call "ventilation." A student wrote about her mother, who she felt was "always defending my brother and sister." Later she told me that it had "felt so good to write the poem, instead of having it stuck inside me." I asked her what she had done to express herself before she wrote about it, and she replied, "I threw things to the ground and got punished for two weeks."

Both therapy and art can spring from difficult and/or bewildering experiences. Sometimes one projects oneself into someone else's place, as a means of understanding and empathizing with that person's situation. Once when I was staying with a group of people in a large house in Vermont, one of the people living there was in an accident. While she lay in critical condition in the hospital (she eventually recovered), her friends tried their best to carry on with their routines. A five-year-old girl was living in the house, and the adults were careful not to talk about the accident while she was around, to "protect" her from the agony everyone else was going through. One night she announced she was going to "put on a play" for us. We gathered in the living room, where she had set up a makeshift stage. The child proceeded to mime the accident, utilizing details everyone thought had been kept from her. At the end of the show she smiled, bowed, and stood there in front of a room full of adults who had been put more in touch with their feelings via a five-year-old's spontaneous use of art. Students can use similar approaches in their writing, either dealing directly with their own experiences or projecting themselves into other people's experiences.

The question is, should we *encourage* students to deal with difficult situations and emotions in their writing, particularly when we notice a student seems upset or we know some fact (a student's parents are getting divorced)? I say — Encourage, no; but, especially when our information comes directly from the student, we can suggest the possibility of writing about it. A good place to start such writing is in the student's personal notebook. Then the student can determine whether to go further with it. A sixth-grader wrote the following notebook entry:

> My parents have been going to court for a year and a half for a divorce, and before that they went to all sorts of marriage counselors. But now it's hurting my brother and I the most. Whenever my dad comes to pick us up and he talks with my mother, I wish he wouldn't, because every time I see them together I wish they would stay married and live together. Or whenever I'm

with one parent I wish I lived with that one, but *sometimes* when I'm with both I wish I was never born.

And an eighth-grader wrote the following:

THAT AUNT OF MINE

An aunt of mine died. Everyone is making a big fuss. Nobody is paying any attention to anyone, except that aunt of mine. Anything that was touched by her is now considered a treasure. So much fuss I hear about her. People ignore me, as if I weren't alive. They make me feel unwanted. They used to treat *me* like a treasure, now like dirt under their feet. Every chance I get I break something of my aunt's. I really used to like her. But now I feel like killing her, even though she's dead. One would think that her death has made me glad, but way down at the bottom of my heart I know I am really sad at the death of that aunt of mine.

Both of these pieces contain thoughts and feelings that might have had no other outlet, and I was glad the writing workshop was an opportunity for the students to air their feelings. In both cases the writing falls into the realm of therapy — literary considerations are secondary to exploring and ventilating personal emotions. In such cases I tell the students that I am aware that the subject matter is delicate and wonder whether he/she would like to pursue it in a more literary manner. If the authors of the above two pieces had chosen to develop their work more, I would have suggested the possibility of writing about themselves in the third person and perhaps changing some essential characteristic(s) — their age, physical appearance, or gender — in order to get some distance and perspective. A short story about a child's hidden response to a death in the family and a story about a child's view of a divorce could result from these beginnings. They would be works of fiction that transcend therapy.

Here is a piece of uncrafted emotion that hasn't been lifted beyond therapeutic release; the writer "shouts" but doesn't get the reader involved in the situation:

I wish I could kill her. I really don't mean it but I do. She hurt me and I'll never forgive her. She told me things that I once believed and now I realize it was all talk. I want to kill myself for believing her but I know that is past and I have to accept it even though I don't want to. I hate myself for it, I hate her for it. If I could just get it off my mind. Every time I see her I think about it.

One response to this piece would be to suggest that the author "lower" her literary voice and let the reader know exactly what is going on. She might also try to write a version from the other person's point of view and perhaps fuse the two versions. Another possibility would be to continue to "shout," but to do it with imagery. The following poem, by another student, may have arisen out of an equally angry situation, but the raw emotions have been channeled into images:

118

I'm seeing you on a long
   noose with your
      hair right out of the water.
I hear you screaming
and cursing at me
but I don't care.
I couldn't because I'm
laughing as you scream.

I see a yacht coming
toward your head and
I take pity
and pull you out.
So now I will go over
and apologize
after hanging you
laughing at you
and drowning you.
Aren't you lucky
I'm compassionate!

                —Cindy Gerbitz

Both of these pieces accomplish something for the writer and have their
place in the workshop, but it's the second one that should be subjected to
critical feedback and/or possible publication.

Therapy And Beyond—Postscript

Sometimes, intense experiences are displaced in art: the emotional content might be transplanted into a different situation or be translated into
metaphor. A homicide detective who was in my adult workshop wrote a
harrowing story about a pack of wild dogs that surrounded and brutalized a
cat. The harsh details and the forcefulness of the writing were such that we
all found ourselves thinking about the story during the week, and as the
next session got underway people resumed talking about it. When I asked
the author what had prompted his writing about the dogs and cat, he realized that he had investigated a murder that resembled the incident in the
story. That particular murder case had upset him a great deal, but he had
been unable to write directly about it — partly because detectives are supposed to be cool about such things—until he found the key to dealing with
the experience metaphorically.

119

8

Shop Talk

DEAR MS. POEMLYHEARTS

Writers care about their craft and though they often have squabbles with it they usually make up and get back together, not unlike many couples. In fact, when I was in graduate school, Kurt Vonnegut, from whom I took a workshop, encouraged me to expand a short story into a novel. After talking about it awhile, he paused and said, "This is like telling you to get married."

Even if you don't get "married" to writing, you can date occasionally, playing the field among poems, stories, diaries, and other forms. Chances are you will then find yourself thinking and talking about writing. Writers, like other workers, enjoy talking shop, and a hefty portion of any shop talk is concerned with problems and difficulties. A typical Vonnegut workshop session would open with him saying, "Well, what problems are we having with our writing — other than not having enough time?"

I tried to think of a way for my students at P.S. 173 in Manhattan to deal with their writing problems that would be instructive and fun. I came up with the idea of having a "Dear Abby"-type column for writers, which we decided to call "Dear Ms. Poemlyhearts; Advice to the Poemlorn" (based on Nathaniel West's novel *Dear Miss Lonelyhearts*). Students could write to "Ms. Poemlyhearts" about serious problems, or they could be playful (it's hard *not* to be satirical in this genre). All letters to Ms. Poemlyhearts were placed in a folder, and anyone could be Ms. Poemlyhearts by selecting and answering one or more letters.

This activity involved communication, satire, and collaboration. I don't know whether the letters and responses actually *helped* anyone, but I suspect that most people read advice columns more for entertainment than for help anyway.

Here is a sampling of Ms. Poemlyhearts letters from P.S. 173 that were originally printed in *Bridge*, the school literary magazine.

(By the way, I didn't write that novel in graduate school. I wasn't ready to settle down.)

DEAR MS. POEMLYHEARTS,

My problem in writing is that sometimes I can't think fast enough. What should I do?

Yours,
SLOW PENCIL

DEAR SLOW,

If you can't think fast enough, DON'T. What I mean is, you don't have to rush. You can take your time writing. Even if you do have a teacher on your back. So take your time.

DEAR MS. POEMLYHEARTS,

What shall I do when my friend keeps asking me to read his poems when I didn't finish my own?

Yours truly,
POEM READER

DEAR POEM R.

Tell him his poem stinks and he will take his poem back right away.
Seriously, take the poem but don't read it. Put it under your poem and finish yours. Then read his poem and make him read yours.

DEAR MS. POEMLYHEARTS,

Whenever I start to write something and show it to my mother and father they always change most of the words. What should I do?

Sincerely,
ALWAYS WRONG

DEAR ALWAYS,

I think you should tell your parents how you feel about that and you should also ask them why they can't just talk to you about what you write instead of changing the words.

121

DEAR MS. POEMLYHEARTS,

I have a very serious problem. I wrote an unpublished book called *She Waits*. It was only for my family to read because it was about some neighbors of mine who aren't married. It had the names of my neighbors with nasty insults about them. I wrote another book, hoping it would get published, called *The Strangler of Noman's Land*. I put it in an envelope to be mailed to Alfred A. Knopf, Inc. A Mr. James Wright called me and said he loved my book *She Waits* and that it would be published. I was so surprised about the call that I didn't listen to the title and gave my permission to publish it. I really like my neighbors and wouldn't want anything to hurt their reputation. The book is now on the Best Sellers List. Is there any way I can stop them from making more copies of the book?

> Please help,
> WORRIED SICK

DEAR WORRIED,

Get yourself a good lawyer. But first let the book sell some more, so you can afford the lawyer.

DEAR MS. POEMLYHEARTS,

What shall I do when I spend a long time thinking about what to write and then I think of an idea and my friend asks me a question? Then I forget my idea.

> Yours truly,
> FORGETFUL
> FRIEND

DEAR FORGETFUL,

Write "screwball" on a piece of paper and show it to your mother. Then she'll hit you on the head and your idea will pop out.

DEAR MS. POEMLYHEARTS,

Every time I sit down to write a poem or story, I read someone else's poem or story to get an idea of what to write, but when I get finished, it ends up just like the one I read to get an idea.

> Thank you,
> IDEALESS INVENTOR

DEAR IDEALESS,

My advice is to think of something that has happened to *you*. Take any event you had and mix it up a little. It's a sure-fire thing.

122

THE GREAT POETRY TEST

It was a fine spring day, my next-to-last session with a high school English class. As I walked into the room, I noticed that half the students had gravitated to the windows, where some were sitting on the radiators, taking in the sun. I wished we could all go outside and remembered that on similar days when I was a student the worst thing that could happen was for the teacher to pull a surprise test.

A strange force came over me and I said, "All right, everyone sit down, clear your desks. Jim, pass out the paper. I'm going to give you 'The Great Poetry Test.' " It was as much news to me as it was to them.

They laughed, saying things like: "There he goes again, checking to see if we're paying attention."

"He's a poet so he thinks he has to say outrageous things."

"A test, right! He doesn't even grade us. Does he?"

But I went through with it—in a way: "I'm going to ask you some questions, and I want you to write down your answers. Have fun with it, but take it seriously—there's no reason you can't do both. I'm not going to grade these, but I will read them carefully."

I made up the questions as I went along. I gave the same "test" to another class that day and subsequently to several other groups at various grade levels, making up a few different questions each time. Most students enjoyed answering the questions. (The only way to "fail" would have been to think any answer could be "wrong.")

My "Great Poetry Test" actually does test something—whether or not I have succeeded with my objective that by the end of a workshop students should be able to write something on demand in a short period of time. To my delight, most students have been able to do some good writing in response to my "test" questions. Here are some questions and sample answers:

1. *What is your image of a poet?**

A poet is a bohemian type who never wears socks and sleeps nude. Preferably thin—or better yet, gaunt—with at least one pierced ear, and dirty fingernails. The poet is not concerned with the appearance of his or her abode, and therefore, it is not uncommon to find week-old pizza crusts strewn about the studio's straw-filled, burlap covered mattress.

A poet can touch things with paper. He also has another job.

A poet is a man inside a man whose brain is illuminated by the fleeting moment and he looks out and in, forming the written image of what was and its residue.

He sees the world through fun house mirrors, distorting even the most obvious and common of everyday occurrences.

---

* This question was borrowed from poet/teacher John Love.

The poet perceives where others dim their minds. He can view a scene where others draw the shade.

A poet is one who has developed his mind and suited it so that he/she is able to organize his innermost thoughts into verbal imagery well enough to be *written* cohesively and creatively.

His appearance is determined by DNA alone.

2. *You say something to someone. They respond, "What?!?!?" What did you say?*

I really love school because they give you a lot of work.

How many times have you taken a swim in the sun?

You say something to someone; they respond, "What?!?!?" What did you say?

3a. *You call your girlfriend, boyfriend, or best friend, excited about some plans, and they say, "I don't want to see you anymore." You hang up the phone. Write an image, short poem, or paragraph describing your reaction.*

The phone cord turns into a snake
which crawls through the receiver
into my ear
down my throat
and into my stomach
where it squirms about
relentlessly.

My hand trembles on the receiver. I am empty and cold. I turn slowly, wishing my mother was there at the doorway so I could run to her. My eyes slowly fill, and my head pounds with bits of words bouncing within it. I pick up the receiver and wish he was still there.

Drinking three pounds of mercury.

3b. *Your friend calls back and says, "I was only kidding." Now how do you feel?*

The sound of a toaster popping up.

The telephone had expanded and filled the room. I crawled under the mouthpiece to answer the phone and when I heard her say, "Just kidding," the phone shrank but I was swallowed into it this time.

My body feels as if someone had shot an arrow through it, then removed the arrow. But it left a deep wound.

4. *Bad things about writing:*

It's never perfect.

People tend to *judge* the work instead of just "feeling" the impressions it was meant to leave you with.

I find it hard to concentrate too much on images and profound expressions.

Words and feelings whirl around in my mind but find no outlet.

Often I write for no one but myself, yet people still find it necessary to criticize.

I know my stuff isn't great and I'm afraid it will never become better.

5. *Good things about writing:*

It makes me more aware of situations and people around me. Things that I might have taken for granted.

I enjoy creating a mood and watching others fall into it. It takes my mind off a problem, although the problem is usually disguised in the writing.

Finally I reveal part of myself that no one else knows; I am understood without feeling vulnerable.

6. *Which of the following celebrities write poetry: Guillermo Vilas, Eugene McCarthy, Richard Thomas, Suzanne Somers, Michael Ontakean, Kareem Abdul Jabbar? (For this question there is a correct answer.)*

All of them (why not?).

7a. *Write two lines that do not have anything to do with each other.*

The speeding light flashed by his eyes.
Twisting and turning in a milk white cocoon.

The bird flew across the sky.
Over my dead body.

7b. *Using no more than three connective words, tie the two lines together.*

The speeding light flashed by his eyes, which sent him
Twisting and turning in a milk white cocoon.

The bird flew across the sky
Over my dead body.

8. *You are looking through a one-way mirror at a writer at work. What do you see?*

He's been sitting in that seat for two hours. Wait, he's getting up and walking over to a light. Now he's darting to his paper and writes furiously. He seems to be finished. He likes it. He likes it a lot. He starts writing again. He is finished

125

with the second one, folds the paper and puts it in his pocket then crumples up the first one and falls asleep in his chair.

It's sort of strange — it's like there's an invisible person there helping him along the way. Suddenly a tear drops from his eye....

9. *You are addressing a group of new teachers. What suggestions would you make for how they teach writing?*

Act like you're a student. Like when you were a student.

You should tell them if a story is good or bad, but never really tell them it stinks. They are only kids.

You have to get the students' attention. Sometimes ask them what kind of writing they would like to do. It would be nice to let them write what they want once in awhile.

CHILDREN TALK ABOUT WRITING

Because people write about things that are important to them, writers write about writing (to use the noun, verb, and gerund in one phrase). The following is a sampling of elementary school students' writings about their work.

Poetry is
a bird
        flying through your open window
when you're half asleep.
You get up
and put it
in a cage
to keep it
        as long as you want
for proof
that it really happened.

                *

I write the things I love.
Love is a big
word and I use it
because it's there to be
used in necessity.
I love to write.
                        —Rebecca Salazar

POETRY

you are caught by a giant
and he is throwing you
out of the world

126

writing on a paper
and it floats in the air

you're pushing a desk
then it goes through
and breaks the wall

a boy breaks into pieces
and you've got to put
him back

—Sarita Santiago

When I write I put my mind
on paper in the form of words,

It's like cracking an egg it
all comes out,

I can almost see the words
weave together

My mind gives the thoughts
My instinct to write makes
them join together to make my
writing build like skyscrapers
that tower above everyone

Sometimes mystery creeps
into my mind to scare me

Writing is almost alive
around me
—Chrissy Keller

I write so that other people can feel good and relaxed, and even excited.
Maybe someday I will be the very, most spectacular poem writer on the sur-
face of this earth. Now I have to cool down and relax myself.
—Jason Ortiz

When you find yourself with nothing to write, you just let yourself go free.
No matter how embarrassing your topic is don't let that worry you. To be a
writer you have to write anything and everything. People like to read embarrassing moments. They'll give you credit. Later on, you'll be very famous.
—Isabel Feliz

9

Workshop Products

PUBLICATIONS

The Literary Magazine. The most appropriate culmination of a writing workshop is a literary magazine. There are several ways of going about it, depending on how much time you want to devote to the project. The quickest route is to ask each student to select one piece of writing and copy it over neatly. Have the material typed, quickly make a cover, run everything through the mimeo machine, and, a few dozen staples later, you have a literary magazine.

BUT...you can also make the magazine an ongoing project which will sharpen students' editorial skills, give them experience in working together, provide them with an alternative activity to writing, and result in a beautiful project which will immortalize the workshop in print.

This kind of magazine takes time, and, if professionally printed, is costly. When there is no money budgeted for a literary magazine, sometimes parents' associations are willing to help. Students might also try the usual fundraising schemes—bakesales, raffles, etc.—or they could offer to list as a "patron" anyone who contributes a certain amount of money. This approach works for the opera and other cultural events; point out to local businesses and other potential supporters that this, too, is a cultural event.

If you have no choice but to do the magazine on a mimeo machine, you can probably scrape up enough money to have the cover printed on card stock. An attractive cover can be designed by doing the title in transfer type (available in art supply and some stationery stores) or calligraphy and by using a line drawing by a student artist. Despite the old saying "You can't judge a book by its cover," a good first impression goes a long way in tempting potential readers to look past the cover.

For most groups, putting together a literary magazine in a democratic way is too unwieldy and time-consuming. The greater the number of students involved, the longer it takes to make decisions. One method I like is to have three student editors in charge of selecting material, and one editor each for design and distribution. I act as coordinating editor to oversee the operation, although at the secondary school level this role too can go to a student. Teachers will vary as to the extent they want to get involved in putting the magazine together, but they should keep the process moving and make sure that the magazine doesn't supplant the workshop's main purpose, which is writing. Although the prospect of publication is one of the incentives for writing, I have had to remind publication-hungry students—who sometimes spend less time writing than talking about the magazine—that the quality of the magazine depends on the quality of their writing.

You and the editorial board will have to make many decisions:

1. Will everyone be included in the publication, or will you pick the best work, even if that means one student may have three pieces and another none? (A compromise is for everyone to be included, but for some students to have more than one selection.)

2. Do you want to include artwork? If so, should drawings illustrate specific writings, or should they be independent of the writing (or a combination of both)? Do you want to involve the art teacher with the magazine or have it emanate totally from the writing workshop? Drawings make good "filler"; after the magazine is laid out, you can add drawings to some pages that have a lot of "white space." Keep in mind that all artwork should be in black ink and drawn to size.

3. How do you want to organize the magazine: by themes (with sections for feelings, dreams, observations); by form (with sections for poems, stories, plays); by author (perhaps alphabetically); by instinct (however it "feels right"); or at random?

4. Do you want an introduction? What should it say? Should it describe the workshop or deal specifically with the contents of the magazine? Who should write it—a student or the teacher? Or should there be an introduction written by both?

5. Should the magazine invite submissions from outside the workshop, from parents, students from other classes, teachers, school staff, or alumni?

6. How will the material be selected? Will the editors go through everyone's folder, or will students be asked to submit self-selected material? What will be the role of the teacher in this process? (You

may want to make the final decisions, with the students acting in an advisory role, or vice versa.)

7. Will the editors make suggestions for revision? If they do, the editorial process can be quite instructive for editors *and* authors, since students are likely to work extra hard on a piece of writing when they know it will be published.

8. How will the magazine be distributed? Who—other than workshop members—will get copies? (If you do not have enough copies for everyone in the school, you can make them available to students on a first-come-first-served basis. Give copies to all teachers, and request that they keep them in their classrooms for perusal by current and future classes; give several to the school library. You can also make the magazine available in the community: local bookstores and the public library may be willing to carry them. Send "review copies" to local newspapers.)

As you can see, putting out a magazine can get quite complicated. Student editors should be cautioned to handle their responsibilities in a sensitive way, since bruised artistic egos can hurt longer than bruised shins.

During most of the school year, I am more concerned with the students' growth as writers than with accumulating work for public display. But when a magazine is being put together, aesthetic criteria come more to the forefront. My pride as a teacher makes me want to see students publish their best work—but students often select inferior material. This may be due to underdeveloped critical faculties or a tendency to play it safe and not publish pieces that are risky in some way. Thus, students may pass over an emotionally or linguistically daring piece for something that is cute or superficial.

When I assert my editorial will, I try to do it in a way that elevates the students' standards, by explaining why I think something is strong. With younger students I sometimes have to remind myself to take into account that even if a particular poem appears childish to me, and less mature than another, the magazine is, after all, by and for children.

No matter how much control the students have over the selection and editing of material, there are two responsibilities the teacher should retain:

1. Check out any material that could be embarrassing to the author or anyone else. Students sometimes reveal personal or family secrets or write something that could hurt a classmate. Readers can be cautioned in the introduction that not everything is objectively true, but this does not eliminate the possibility that a piece of writing could cause some damage. Discuss any touchy pieces with the authors, making sure they understand the possible ramifications of publication. You will have to decide whether to leave the final decision up to the author or make it yourself, which you may want to do when someone other than the

author is involved. This is an extremely knotty problem even for professional writers, whose relatives and friends often populate their writings, not always in flattering ways.

2. Make sure nothing gets published containing grammatical errors, misspellings, or blatant lapses in writing. There has been long debate among writing teachers as to the extent — if any — we should alter students' writings. Some have mistakenly confused a well-intentioned desire not to tamper with the integrity of students' writings with a reluctance to give their students the same courtesy any editor would extend to an author. I would feel let down if an editor allowed something of mine to be published with a grammatical error or misspelling or if he/she didn't call my attention to any other questionable points. Sometimes what looks like "bad writing" is a result of an error in copying a piece over.

Students work very hard on, and often feel emotionally attached to, their writings, and I would hate for anyone to bring home the magazine and, instead of hearing about what a wonderful poem he/she has written, be corrected on a grammatical point.

As for nongrammatical changes, when possible I discuss my suggestions with students and leave the final decision up to them. But often a publication has to be rushed into print in order to be out by the end of the school year, and I don't have the time to work closely with the authors or student editors. I then make the selections for the magazine myself and prepare the copy for the typist. I do not make any changes that violate the voice of the piece in order to make it "better," but I may eliminate a redundancy or a particularly bad line, and, in some cases, will "tighten" a phrase if I am sure that such a change is not beyond the student's own capability.

Other Publications. In addition to the literary magazine, you can publish *chapbooks* of work by individual students. Defined as a "small book," the chapbook format is widely used by small literary publishers. For your purposes, a chapbook can be 8–16 pages long and contain poems, stories, or one long piece. Students can put together manuscripts of their own work and submit them either to you or a committee of students. Those whose work isn't selected could make covers for their manuscripts, thus turning them into "limited editions of one."

Another form of publication is the *broadside*—a single sheet containing one or more pieces of writing. Sometimes I have quickly produced broadsides on 8½ " × 11 " (or 14 ") paper, cramming in as many pieces as possible from a particularly successful workshop session. Other times, I use the broadside for a single piece I think is worthy of immediate distribution. The broadside can be mimeographed, photocopied, or printed. Using transfer type for the title and a line drawing to accompany the writing can make a broadside quite appealing.

A Note On Typos. Every author and editor knows that gremlins live inside typewriters and typesetting machines. These gremlins have the power to turn a "thus" into a "thud" and make a "nose" out of a "rose." But the most devilish thing about these gremlins is that they coat some of their little pranks with a substance that enables them to elude the probing of proofreaders. Students should be warned that most publications include typos, and one or more can strike any poem or story. Some typos aren't very harmful ("thr" for "the"), while other typos actually alter the meaning, and although writers may not grin they have no choice but to bear them. "Welcome to the club," I tell students who complain of typos in their work. Norman Mailer, when he was writing a column for *The Village Voice,* found that his phrase "the nuances of growth" appeared in print as "the nuisances of growth." Nuisances, indeed; the gremlins must have really enjoyed that one.

PERFORMANCES

Although publication is the writer's main medium for sharing work, it is not the only one. Poetry and prose readings offer writers the direct contact with their audience that is lacking in publications. An immediate facial or vocal response from someone who is touched, amused, or inspired by a reading can buoy a writer's spirits. Readings can be stiff, formal, and dull, but they don't have to be. Robin Messing, a colleague working at Waverly Park School in Lynbrook, Long Island, has produced two exciting events with her fifth-grade students. One year, the students did a cabaret-style poetry reading. Assisted by a few parents, they turned the gym into a "café." Parents sat with their children at small tables set with plates of cookies and cups of juice. Each student read a poem at the microphone. Intermittently, the school band played a few tunes.

The following year Robin and her class put on a "poetry parade." Using colored magic markers, each student made two copies of one of his/her poems on large, white construction paper; many added illustrations. As Robin described it, "The white papers were then pasted onto large colored papers, which served as frames for the poems. We punched holes at the top and threaded yarn through the holes to be tied around the children's necks." Thus, the children could wear their poems on sandwich board signs —like the kind in the cartoons that say "Eat At Joe's"—reaching down as far as their ankles. The students made paper hats, and, accompanied by a few members of the school band, embarked on their poetry parade. With the band playing, the group marched into classrooms (teachers were notified in advance) and formed a circle around the children. Several students read in each class, separated by the beating of the drums. With the announcement "This has been your poetry parade," the band struck up a tune and the colorful troupe marched on, leaving behind a slightly bewildered but impressed group of students.

As I watched, I was moved by the assertiveness of the event. Many people think of writing as an isolated, "quiet" act. Poetry is rarely grist for bragging among youngsters: "I can write better poems than you!" "Oh yeah? Sez who?" The poetry parade, in its bravado, carried the message that a writer's place does not have to be in the closet.

You need not be as elaborate as Robin to put on student poetry readings. Students can read, without trappings, for each other. Or, they can go into other classes, following their readings with questions from the audience. Generally, each student shouldn't read for more than a few minutes at a time.

I advise students to read slightly slower than they think they should, to enunciate clearly without sounding "phony," and to read with the conviction that "this is my writing and I am sure of the sanctity and utter importance of every line (or at least I will read it as if I were sure)."

"Don't be nervous" is not necessarily a good piece of advice. While it is certainly not helpful to be paralyzed by nerves, a few butterflies floating around before a reading often metamorphose into an energizing force during the performance.

Video Tape. Some schools have video-tape equipment, which can be put to use by the workshop. A video tape of students reading their work and discussing writing can be played for other classes in the school and for subsequent workshops.

Appendix

FOUR STUDENTS*

Michael. Michael, a sixth-grader, was a problem. He could be disruptive; and worse, he could get mean. Once when a girl called him a liar, he responded by grabbing the play she had been working on and ripping it into shreds. A less hostile act would have been to hit her. The word "liar" had riled up demons living deep inside him. "*Never* call me a liar," he hissed as he clenched the shredded paper.

Later in the year, a few of the boys in my workshop decided to write and sing their own songs. Michael walked into the room during a rehearsal and announced he was joining. No one objected; Michael's glare told them they had no choice. I shuddered, and hoped that Michael's demons liked to sing. Michael took the mike and started improvising a song, and soon the others fell in as his back-up group. Michael had a good voice and feeling for lyrical and melodic structure. He took over the role of disciplinarian from me, allowing for less fooling around than I had and insisting that the focus stay on the work.

I told the principal about Michael's singing and songwriting, adding that he should be "up on a stage." The principal replied, "How about under a stagecoach?"

---

*The names of the first two students have been changed.

"This is a different Michael," I said. "I've never seen him like this."

At one session, Michael asked my colleague Cliff Safane to play some "sad music" on the piano: "You know, like when your momma's died." Cliff played and Michael sang along:

My momma's gone
I'm alone
I need someone
To turn to
I need someone to turn to
Can I turn to you?

About ten years ago
My momma used to say to me,
"Listen, Michael, stay and pray
Do good in school
Keep out of trouble"
Sometimes I've been bad
Sometimes I wish I had
My mother

Mother
Mommy

Michael graduated, and a year later I heard a rumor that he had been suspended from junior-high school for hitting a teacher. There's no great moral to this story, other than that writers and other artists are sometimes troubled people who are able to put their demons to constructive work.

Creative writing can give otherwise unsuccessful students a shot at achieving self-satisfaction while also excelling at something in school. I don't expect lives to change as a result; this is not a TV series, where the writing teacher visits the problem-student's home and the parents say, "Sit down and have dinner, you've done *so much* for our child. Can we ask one more favor? Please go with him when he signs his recording contract." But I do try to keep my eyes—and heart—open for the kid who, despite acting in ways that I don't like, might like to write.

Betty. During the writing segment of my third session with a fourth-grade class, I asked the teacher if there were any students with writing problems whom I hadn't noticed. She pointed me toward a girl with shiny hair, Betty. I noticed her hair because it covered her face and the paper in front of her. I walked over and saw that the paper was blank. I asked her if she was having problems or was just thinking, but she didn't answer. When she finally spoke, the words were slurred—a speech impediment or shyness?

I ignored other demands on my attention and stayed with Betty. A challenge. She told me she had nothing to write about, so I asked her if there was anything or anyone she felt strongly about, either love, hate, disgust, or attraction. Finally, she confided that she did like her mother and her cat. After a few more minutes of conversation she wrote a simple little poem about her mother and cat. Betty and I had both met the challenge. The teacher was impressed.

During succeeding visits, Betty became more than a challenge. I got to like her, and she was getting attached to me. We had long talks, and since Betty didn't talk much in school, the teacher was anxious to know what we talked about: Did we talk about her family situation? Rumor had it that her mother had a new boyfriend. Actually, Betty and I didn't talk about very important things; it was just important that we talked.

When I saw Betty in the halls, she would run up to me, smiling. One morning I saw her at the other end of the hall. She didn't see me. A boy accidentally bumped into her and shouted to his friends, "Someone get me the cooty gun! Betty touched me! Hurry, the cooties are all over me." Betty heard this but continued on her way without changing her expression.

I was bothered both by the cruelty of the boy's comments and by Betty's nonreaction; could this be a common experience? Perhaps it tore at her inside but she couldn't let it come to the surface without making herself even more vulnerable.

I resolved to speak highly of Betty in the hearing of other students, to use my position of prestige to heighten her class standing. I wanted very badly for Betty to write terrific poems so I could read them to the class. But Betty did not write terrific poems. She tried hard, but perhaps she was simply not capable of it. "A learning disability," the teacher called it, a phrase that had always struck me as a possibly self-fulfilling prophecy. Betty did her best and improved, though she still did not write terrific poems.

One day right before the bell rang I was critical of Betty's poem, thinking she had become complacent due to my constant support. When I returned to the classroom a few minutes later to tell the teacher something, I noticed that Betty was crying. I went over and asked her if I had said something that had hurt her.

"I hate you," she whispered, and stared at her desk. I remembered the "cooty gun" incident, afraid that I had become one more tormentor for her. However, I convinced myself that she said she hated me because she was afraid she liked me too much. Still, I felt badly.

The teacher said to me, "Betty cries a lot. Always tears. The best thing is to ignore them. She'll be okay in a few minutes. Oh, I heard that her mother is getting married again and they're moving soon."

Later that day, I saw Betty in the remedial reading room, a place where she always seemed more at ease. I asked her if it was true that she was moving. She began to cry again.

Lisa. Lisa Burris was a constant. For three years (from fourth through sixth grades) no matter what was going on in the writing workshop, through distractions and conflicts, Lisa shone. She took care of her business. Even when she was struggling, she enjoyed writing. She was perfectly capable of fooling around with the other kids, but she always settled down and got her writing done. If only *I* had her discipline.

136

In addition to being in a writing workshop, sometimes Lisa came to my room to write in her notebook while I was busy with something else. One day she seemed particularly happy with a poem she had written.

PROMISES

My mother made
a great promise.
My father made one,
too.
They both promised
me to stop quarreling.
At least for a little
while.
My cousin made
a promise,
my uncle and aunt
too.
But they all broke
their promises one
by one.
I don't want a perfect
family who would always
dress up fancy and neat.
Just a family that keeps
a promise,
altogether,
one.

Sometimes students "write well" but the writing has no life to it—the bones are assembled in the correct formation, the features are properly positioned, but the poor creature has a blank expression, can't laugh or cry, sing or dance. As writing teachers, what kind of experience do we want for our students? A good experience with writing—the feeling that there was some reason to take pen to paper—should be right up there on top of any list of our goals. Sometimes this good experience comes from a nutty, sur-realistic romp through language; sometimes it's a skillful manipulation of words that has the effect of depicting an observation or experience. And sometimes, as in the case of the poem "Promises" by Lisa, it's a direct rendering of a state of feeling, getting something off your chest and onto paper, via your mind. Is Lisa's a good poem? I don't want to think about that right now. Was it a good writing experience? She thought it was.

I read the poem to another class. They listened, quietly, caught up in the words.

Gerry. What happens to students after we leave each other: what is the long-term effect of the workshop? How much do they remember? Too often, I never know. But occasionally I cross paths with former students and we renew our acquaintance, and others keep in touch with letters, sometimes stuffed with new poems. The student who has stayed in touch with me the longest is Gerry Pearlberg.

When she was in ninth grade, Gerry came to my poetry workshop by mistake. She had thought it would be a short story class. She had never written poetry, but decided to give it a try, and went on to become the most prolific, and perhaps the most talented, student I have ever had. In addition to the workshop, we met in a tutorial setting, and at the end of the year, Teachers & Writers published a small book of her poems, *Night Quiver*. Gerry participated in every step of the process, including a visit to the typesetters. I sent a copy of her book to a well-known poet, who replied, "My goodness, a book at 14;...I hope she's a strong girl as well as being talented. At 14 she's got a long way to go, and most of the journey she's got to be able to make herself." I thought about this. What had I gotten her into? Or, more accurately, what had I helped her get herself into? Yes, she would have to be strong, but there would always be teachers, friends, other poets, and, in moments of solitude, language.

Gerry's letters and our conversations over the years have included moments of excitement and doubt about her writing. She has also expressed indecision regarding whether to make a go of it as a writer or to pursue another profession and write on the side. As a college freshman, she wrote to me:

> I know what my goals & needs are—minimal material wealth (just as long as I always have enough $ for a bandana). But what I don't really know is crucial: Am I good enough (as a writer)? I don't know. Maybe it's too soon to tell....I like what I write, I read a lot, I devote a great part of myself & my time & energy to writing....So it's part of me & life, but does that mean I should choose it as a vocation?

I replied that she didn't have to make that decision yet, since either way she planned to continue college, and it never hurts a writer to learn as much as possible about anything and everything. She could (and should) keep her options open. The following year, writer's block hit. She didn't stop writing entirely, but the little she wrote didn't seem "real or interesting" to her. And to make matters worse, she feared she might be letting me down: "It's not that I think you think I owe you anything, some tangible *result*....But my self-expectations are being strained by all this."

I reassured her that my friendship did not have to be paid for in verse. If she never wrote another line, I would be grateful for the pleasure I have received from what she had already written. A couple of months later, I received a letter full of news about courses and activities. Plus:

> I've eased back into a writing spirit, too....it feels good to be back with poetry, to be having psychedelic dreams, to be thinking of everything as something else, to be enjoying colors and shadows and puddles and night again. My work is taking a lot of new directions, which is simultaneously exhilarating and frightening, because it almost seems out of my control. So

when was it ever in my control, really? . . . . It's just strange to see that voice saying things it never said before in different ways from before.

THE VISITING WRITER

Such programs as Teachers & Writers Collaborative and Poets-in-the-Schools (funded by the National Endowment for the Arts and individual state arts councils) enable writers to visit classrooms to preach what they practice. It can be for a short-term series of workshops (six to ten visits) or a long-term residency. The following notes can enhance the relationship between visiting writer and teacher.

Meet with the writer before he/she starts working with your students. This should go beyond a perfunctory hello and setting up of schedules. A pre-program planning session can include the following:

1. Ask the writer questions about his/her work and background. Rather than considering this an invasion of privacy, most writers enjoy talking about themselves and will take your questions as a sign of interest.

2. Ask how the students should be prepared for the residency: what they should be told about it, whether there are any writing exercises the class can do in advance.

3. Tell the writer of any special projects you have been working on and particular areas the class has been studying (such as "immigration" or "American Indians") in case he/she might want to prepare a related writing assignment or bring in writing that deals with the subject.

4. Find out how the writer wants to be introduced to the group. Many writers prefer to be called by their first names, while others prefer the more formal "Mr.," "Ms.," or "Mrs."

5. Discuss classroom procedures. Let the writer know what is acceptable and what is forbidden in your classroom. Perhaps he/she will request that some rules—such as a rule requiring that students not leave their seats without permission — be suspended during the workshop. If there is a conflict between a classroom policy and the way the writer wants to run the workshop, one solution is to tell the class that since these writing sessions are different from other classroom activities certain changes will be in effect for the duration. I have been in situations where I unknowingly gave permission to a student to break a teacher's rule, and then heard the student say to the teacher, "But the writer *said* I could!" Situations like this can cause antagonisms to fester, so discuss potential problem areas in advance.

Have the class prepared for each session. If possible, allow the students a few minutes' breather before the writer gets there, giving them a chance to

139

sharpen their pencils, clear their desks, and go to the bathroom. Unless the writer requests otherwise, pass out writing paper in advance. Avoid scheduling tests right before the workshop session.

These may seem like small points, but when a writer is working under the severe time pressure of a short-term residency squeezed into 45-minute periods every minute counts. It is disconcerting to walk into a classroom where students are hurriedly finishing a math test, followed by a flurry of pencil sharpening, paper passing, and requests to go to the bathroom.

Convey to the class your approval and enthusiasm for the program. Students will be asked to do work that is not part of their routine, and your "sanction" will make it easier for the writer to make demands on them. Your continued interest in what they are writing will not only help the writer, but will make it easier for you to continue the work after the residency is completed.

Follow up between visits. Ask the writer if he/she would like you to allot some time between visits for the students to revise and/or copy over their work from the previous session. In a short-term residency, revision is the part of the writing process most likely to fall by the wayside. Students often are not able to do more than a first draft during the workshop period, and writers often go on to something new each session in order to give the students a wide range of experiences.

If the writer gives the class a home assignment, remind the class about the assignment a day or two before the next session. Ask the writer if he/she has any other ideas for what you can do between visits. It is difficult to maintain momentum, especially when there is a week between sessions. You can keep the spirit alive by discussing the writing sessions.

Help out during sessions. Some writers prefer the teacher not to get very involved, while others like it when the teacher asks questions or makes suggestions during the lesson. All would prefer teachers to pay attention, rather than grade papers or read the newspaper, activities which can communicate to the students that you don't have high regard for the workshop.

While the students are writing, the writer might want you to walk around the room, answering questions and offering advice. Again, the best procedure is to communicate with the writer, so you don't feel that you are either intruding on the workshop process by participating or ignoring what is going on by not participating.

Help the writer feel at home. Let him/her in on any tips, such as the best place to get coffee or lunch, where the faculty bathrooms are, and how to go about getting something mimeographed. If the writer is from out of town and is spending a week in the community, an offer for a drink after school or a home-cooked meal can be welcome. (Most writers aren't the "lonely, starving artist" types.)

About the Author

ALAN ZIEGLER, a poet and prose writer, has been teaching writing workshops, mostly for Teachers & Writers Collaborative, since 1974. His students have ranged from age seven to adult. He is Writers' Coordinator of Teachers & Writers Collaborative and coordinates Writers-in-Lynbrook, a district-wide program of creative writing workshops in Lynbrook, Long Island. He has taught for Poets-in-the-Schools, Poets & Writers, and Bronx Community College of the City University of New York and has worked as a journalist.

Mr. Ziegler has conducted seminars, consulted, and given talks on the teaching of writing for the NCTE (National Council of Teachers of English), NIE (National Institute of Education), Vassar College, Adelphi University, Loyola University, Hamilton College, Hampshire College, the New York City Board of Education, and others. He has worked extensively with teachers, and his articles on teaching writing have appeared in *Teachers & Writers Magazine, The Whole Word Catalogue II,* and *Journal of a Living Experiment.* Poetry by his students comprises the text of *Almost Grown,* a book of photographs of teenagers by Joseph Szabo.

Mr. Ziegler is the author of *So Much To Do* (poems and prose poems), *Planning Escape* (poems), and *Sleeping Obsessions* (collaborative poems with Harry Greenberg and Larry Zirlin). His poetry and prose have appeared in such publications as *Paris Review, The Ardis Anthology of New American Poetry, The Village Voice, American Poetry Review, Poetry Now,* and *Carolina Quarterly.* He has given many readings of his work and is co-editor of *Some* literary magazine. He has a masters degree in creative writing from The City College of New York, where he studied with Kurt Vonnegut and Joel Oppenheimer.

Kipling, Rudyard. "Working-Tools." In *The Writer's Craft*, edited by John Hersey. New York: Alfred A. Knopf, Inc., 1975.

Lloyd, David. "An Interview with James Tate." In *Durak* magazine, 1979.

Lopate, Phillip. "Helping Young Children Start to Write." In *Research on Composing: Points of Departure,* edited by Charles R. Cooper and Lee Odell. Urbana, Ill.: National Council of Teachers of English, 1978.

May, Rollo. *The Courage to Create.* New York: Bantam Books, Inc., 1976.

Mayakovsky, Vladimir. *How Are Verses Made?* London: Jonathan Cape, 1970.

Mencken, H. L. *The American Language.* New York: Alfred A. Knopf, Inc., 1979.

Mills, Ralph J., Jr., ed. *The Notebooks of David Ignatow.* Chicago: The Swallow Press, Inc., 1973.

Mozart, Wolfgang Amadeus. A letter. In *Creativity,* edited by P. E. Vernon. New York: Penguin Books, 1970.

Murray, Donald M. "Internal Revision: A Process of Discovery." In *Research on Composing: Points of Departure,* edited by Charles R. Cooper and Lee Odell. Urbana, Ill.: National Council of Teachers of English, 1978.

O'Hara, Frank. "Statement on Poetics." In *The New American Poetry,* edited by Donald M. Allen. New York: Grove Press, Inc., 1960.

Olson, Charles. *Selected Writings.* New York: New Directions Publishing Corporation, 1966.

Preminger, Alex, ed. *Princeton Encyclopedia of Poetry and Poetics.* Princeton, N.J.: Princeton University Press, 1974.

Shaughnessy, Mina P. *Errors and Expectations: A Guide for the Teacher of Basic Writing.* New York: Oxford University Press, 1977.

Shore, Michael. "An Interview with Rodney Dangerfield." In *Soho News,* 1979.

Tchaikovsky, Peter Ilyich. Letters. In *Creativity,* edited by P. E. Vernon. New York: Penguin Books, 1970.

Tolstoy, Leo. "What is Art?" In *The Writer's Craft,* edited by John Hersey. New York: Alfred A. Knopf, Inc., 1975.

Wagner, Linda, ed. *Interviews with William Carlos Williams—Speaking Straight Ahead.* New York: New Directions Publishing Corporation, 1976.

Whittemore, Reed. *William Carlos Williams: Poet from New Jersey.* Boston: Houghton Mifflin Company, 1975.

Williams, William Carlos. "A New Measure." In *Modern Poetics,* edited by James Scully. New York: McGraw-Hill, Inc., 1965.

Williams, William Carlos. *I Wanted to Write a Poem: The Autobiography of the Works of a Poet.* New York: New Directions Publishing Corporation, 1977.

BIBLIOGRAPHY

Given the nature of this book's subject matter, it is not always possible to pinpoint the source of an idea because some of the ideas have evolved from discussions with colleagues. I apologize if there are any omissions.

Auden, W. H. "Writing." In *The Poet's Work,* edited by Reginald Gibbons. Boston: Houghton Mifflin Company, 1979.

Bartlett, Elsa Jaffe. "Learning to Write" (A Report to the Ford Foundation). New York: 1980.

Benedikt, Michael, ed. *The Prose Poem: An International Anthology.* New York: Dell Publishing Company, 1976.

Berg, A. Scott. *Max Perkins—Editor of Genius.* New York: Pocket Books, 1979.

Bly, Robert, ed. *The Seventies.* Madison, Minn.: The Seventies, 1972.

Burnett, Hallie and Burnett, Whit. *Fiction Writer's Handbook.* New York: Harper & Row Publishers, 1975.

Deutsch, Babette. *Poetry Handbook.* New York: Grosset & Dunlap, Inc., 1962.

Flaubert, Gustave. Letters to Louise Colet. In *The Writer's Craft,* edited by John Hersey. New York: Alfred A. Knopf, Inc., 1975.

Freud, Sigmund. "Creative Writers and Day-Dreaming." In *Creativity,* edited by P.E. Vernon. New York: Penguin Books, 1970.

Funk, Wilfred. *Word Origins and their Romantic Stories.* New York: Crown Publishers, Inc., 1978.

Hayden, Robert. "The Poet and His Art: A Conversation." In *How I Write.* New York: Harcourt Brace Jovanovich, Inc., 1972.

Heller, Erich, ed. *The Basic Kafka.* New York: Pocket Books, 1979.

Housman, A. E. "The Name and Nature of Poetry." In *The Writer's Craft,* edited by John Hersey. New York: Alfred A. Knopf, Inc., 1975.

Hugo, Richard. *The Triggering Town: Lectures and Essays on Poetry and Writing.* New York: W. W. Norton & Company, Inc., 1979.

Jacob, Max. *Advice to a Young Poet.* London: Menard Press, 1976.

Jung, C. G. *The Spirit in Man, Art, and Literature.* Translated by R.F.C. Hull. Princeton, N.J.: Princeton University Press, 1971.

Conflicts. Ironically, conflicts between writer and teacher sometimes occur when teachers themselves are actively involved in teaching writing. This may be because the teacher feels that the writer is invading his/her "turf," possibly with some ideas about writing that differ from what he/she has been telling the class. Whatever the reason, it's a shame when this happens.

Conflicting views about writing can be confusing to students, but they should be presented in the context of increasing their options rather than obscuring "the truth." There is no right or wrong way to think about many aspects of writing. Poet Louis Ginsberg, in discussing how his attitudes toward poetry sometimes differed from those of his son, Allen, said, "There are many rooms in the house of poetry."

An uncomfortable situation can also occur when the writer and teacher are in *agreement*. I've had the experience of presenting a lesson to a class and afterwards hearing the teacher tell me, "Well, we already did *that*," as if I was supposed to come up with completely new things to say about writing because I am an expert. It is much more advantageous for the writer and teacher to see themselves as partners.

I preface my comments to other people's students by saying, "I might be reinforcing some things you've already heard, but maybe I'll add a different twist to it. And if I contradict what you've heard before, let me know, and we'll discuss it. Maybe it's a paradox rather than a contradiction."

SEGUE TO VOLUME TWO

No matter how conducive an atmosphere for writing you create with your students, no matter how much the students understand the writing process, times will come — and they will come often — when you will hear the question: "But what are we supposed to write today?"

See you next volume.